Do Epic Sh*t

Kicking Butt before
Kicking the Bucket

SARA RUTHNUM

DEDICATION

To my mum, dad, sister and friends.

To Bart and Jason for all their encouragement
and support along the way.

And to the bucket list adventures still yet to be had.

CONTENTS

ACKNOWLEDGEMENTS

I have so many great people to thank for their continued support of this book.

Do Epic Sh*t would not have been possible to write without the support and mentorship of Bart Wisniowski and Jason Lindstrom. From the outline, to the content, to coming up with a title that truly represent the book, your support and guidance has helped me to achieve one of the most humbling bucket list goals. Thank you for all of your amazing leadership, patience, and encouragement while this book has come to life. I can whole-heartedly say I could not have done this without your help.

Secondly, I'd like to thank you, Bart and Jason, for all your hard work and dedication in making the world a more accomplished and fulfilled place through Bucketlist.org.

To my friends and family, it's because of you that I have been instilled with the desire and passion to experience the world, and all it has to offer.

Finally, to the Bucketlist community, thank you for sharing your incredible successes and achievements with me. Everyday I am astounded by your accomplishments and devotion to achieving extraordinary adventures.

I am truly inspired every day to come to work.

PREFACE

What do you want to do in your life?

Everyone has a bucket list. Every single person on this planet has hopes and dreams, plans and expectations, and undoubtedly amazing aspirations. Some have it hidden in the back of their minds, while others have it pasted on their bathroom mirror, repeating it methodically, envisioning their future at every waking moment of the day. Everyone has a bucket list.

When we begin to find ourselves in a routine, it becomes easy to let the mind wander and think, "One day I wish…." Or, "Someday I'm going to," lusting over Pinterest boards of exotic locations and adventurous activities we hope to one day experience for ourselves. But when the bills begin to roll in, and the responsibilities pile on, the dreams on your life's list are easily pushed aside for reality.

But when is it enough? When do we decide the value of our experiences is just as important as the traditional sense of stability? Why does it always have to be in the future? Let's stop with the excuses and start living, today. I'll admit that it is *always* easier said than done, but hear me out. There's really no time like the present to start living for your dreams, because the only mistake you'll make is not working towards your goals sooner. But if you still need a little convincing to get out there, sit back and enjoy this ultimate guide to achieving your goals and get ready to discover, plan, and crush your bucket list.

From travelling the globe to exploring the micro-adventures in your surroundings, it's time to start achieving and succeeding. Take a moment, and read the wise words of Stephen Sutton:

> *"Imagine there is a bank account that credits your account each morning with $86,400. It carries over no balance from day to day. Every evening the bank deletes whatever part of the balance you failed to use during the day. What would you do? Draw out every penny, of course!*
>
> *Each of us has such a bank. Its name is TIME. Every morning, it credits you with 86,400 seconds. Every night it writes off as lost, whatever of this you have failed to invest to a good purpose. It carries over no balance. It allows no over draft. Each day it opens a new account for you. If you fail to use the day's deposits, the loss is yours."* - Stephen Sutton [1]

Time. We have to start thinking of time as the true currency of life. How do you want to remember your life when you're 90 years old, sitting in the old folks home? I want to live the kind of life I can be proud of. I want to see the far corners of

[1] http://www.stefanwissenbach.com/articles/finding-the-value-in-86400-seconds-stephens-story.php

the earth, and do the types of things that make my heart beat faster just by reminiscing.

From age 8 to 80, I hope you'll find the information in this book inspiring and motivating to help you take your first steps to live a truly bucket list worthy life.

"The only impossible journey is the one you never begin."
– Anthony Robbins

It's time for you to get up and start living; to brush off the monotony of routine, and become that person who seems to have it all together, because you do. It's time for you to start investing those precious 86,400 seconds into your life.

No one's going to plan your life for you, and only you can decide you're ready to chase your dreams and live a satisfied and fulfilled life. This book is for the person who's ready to put the living back in life. The ambitious person, the adventurous person, the wild child and the bookworm; this book is for you.

What this book will cover

"I don't have the time."

"I don't have the money."

"I just don't know what to do."

Sound familiar? In this book I'm going to show you how to overcome these obstacles step by step. First, I will break down the most popular types of bucket list goals, such as travel, adventure, skills and personal development. Then, in the second part, take a look at what you need to do before your adventure, like saving money, what you need to organize and plan, and how to take the first step in your adventurous life. With the majority of our bucket list goals being travel related, I compiled, in the third section, a guide to kick-starting your travel and adventure dreams.

Finally, I'll look at some of the incredible bucket list goals from our community and how real people like you have gone about achieving them.

PART 1

Breaking Down a Bucket List
One Goal at a Time

"Nothing can stop the man with the right mental attitude from achieving his goal; nothing on earth can help the man with the wrong mental attitude."

- Thomas Jefferson

INTRODUCTION

Kicking Butt before Kicking the Bucket

Decide what it is you want.
Write that shit down.
Make a plan.
And...
Work on it.
Every.
Single.
Day.

This book isn't called *Do Average Sh*t* or *Do Normal Sh*t* – that might be a book about pooping. This is *Do Epic Sh*t* for EPIC people wanting to live EPIC lives. I don't want to scare away people who don't want to describe their lives as extreme, because, truthfully, I'm about the furthest person away from extreme. So when I use the word epic to describe life, I really am saying prideful and fulfilled, but that doesn't have the same ring to it "Someday dreaming" is all fine and well, but there's no time like today to get your sh*t together. One day it clicked for me. Why does it always have to be in the future, why not now? Well the biggest reasons – excuses

– I used to say everyday were, "I don't have the money," "I don't have the time," or, "I don't know what to do." So I did nothing. They all seemed like valid reasons at the time, yet I had enough money to go out for dinner frequently and buy that new outfit. Something wasn't quite adding up. I always wanted to live the life of legends, but I didn't know where to start. These are the typical problems of a 20-something-year-old.

This book doesn't have all the answers – I'm not Oprah – but it is a start. From countless hours of research, to pulling from some of my own adventures and life stories/experiences, I'm going to share with you the secrets to accomplishing your life goals, with help from the team at Bucketlist HQ. We're not just talking about what you kind of hoped to do one day. We're talking about actionable steps to achieve your ever-growing bucket list, which come from people like you who cross off achievements from their bucket list every day.

A little bit about Bucketlist and me

You might be thinking, 'Who is this girl telling me what to do with my life?' I get it. Bucket lists can be *deeply* personal and a bit of a touchy subject. Well, as weird as it sounds, bucket lists have sort of become my thing. For the last year or so of my life, I have been immersed in everything that bucket lists have to offer. In fact, I actually work for Bucketlist, a company dedicated to helping people discover, support, and achieve their life ambitions. Every day I get to talk with over-accomplished, amazingly inspiring people, who share their stories and adventures. I get to research exotic locations, and I get to write about my own fumbling experiences achieving my bucket list.

More than that, I get to uncover some of the most extreme bucket list ideas from over 3 million goals and counting, read and share from over 400,000 successfully accomplished bucket list goals, and connect with people from the Bucketlist community, which has grown to over 200,000 amazing individuals around the world. As you can see, bucket lists are weirdly my thing.

Being in this incredibly unique position, I knew I had an opportunity to not only help others live a fulfilled life, but also uncover the mystery and popularity of bucket lists. In the next chapter you'll see the upward trend of goal setting in the modern age and how bucket lists have progressed to be, essentially, a modern day phenomena. For this book, I dove deep into the data from our site to see the trends and insights our information showed. Unlike some inspirational books, I wanted to use real research and numbers to uncover the truth in bucket lists, and how you can get on the path to success in all aspects of your life. And, of course, most importantly, I want to share some astonishing stories of everyday people accomplishing their epic dreams.

But before I get too far ahead of myself, let's start at the beginning. What is a bucket list?

What is a Bucket List?

Bucket lists have become engrained in our society, with everyone from President Obama to Neil Patrick Harris to Oprah talking about their lists and making the news. It's hard to go a week without hearing of a heart-wrenching, tear-jerking news story of someone trying to accomplish his or her life list before something devastating happens. These bucket list stories are compelling and relatable because, as I said before, everyone has a bucket list. The media almost obsessively publicizes when a notable person makes mention of their bucket list. It is extremely fascinating to see these already incredibly high achieving individuals still striving for more. The beauty of a bucket list is that it transcends power, cultures, and stereotypes.

The most recent example would have to be from former President Bill Clinton. He has seen some of the most remote corners of the earth, met with heads of states and celebrities, not to mention he was the president of the United States of America, and yet he has a bucket list. His most newsworthy answer when asked, "What's on your bucket list?" was to "ride a horse across the Gobi Desert to the place where people think Genghis khan is buried in Mongolia.[2]" Bucket lists aren't limited to your age, income bracket, or successes; no matter who you are, you should keep striving for more.

Let's take a closer look at the term "Bucket List." Where did it come from? How is it used today? If we look back 20 years ago, the term was virtually unheard of, but now bucket lists have become a phenomenon. I'm definitely not a scholar or linguist by any means, but I did scour quite a few resources to come up with an explanation.

The term bucket list originates from the saying to kick the bucket, which is considered slang for – to be blunt – dying, and there are several theories why. These theories vary. One idea is that it came from a method of execution where they used to hang people and would make the person stand on an upside down bucket. When it was kicked, that meant the end of their life. Another idea proposes it is referencing the

---

[2] http://www.mediabistro.com/fishbowldc/whats-on-a-former-presidents-bucket-list-bill-clinton-dishes-to-mike-allen_b134652

children's game of kick the can. But I like to think of a bucket list as a guide for living an exceptional life.

The term is popular amongst a variety of cultures speaking different languages and several sources online indicate it has been in use since the early/mid 2000s. Though, it became popularized as a household term after the movie *The Bucket List* came out (great movie by the way). In case you're not familiar, *The Bucket List* is about two terminally ill friends embarking on a journey to complete a bucket list before time runs out.

> *"You know, the ancient Egyptians had a beautiful belief about death. When their souls got to the entrance to heaven, the guards asked two questions. Their answers determined whether they were able to enter or not. 'Have you found joy in your life?' 'Has your life brought joy to others?'"* – The Bucket List

Now, a bucket list typically will contain ideas, experiences, and achievements that are worthy of a hearty discussion with good friends and are a chronicle of everything you have done, and all the remarkable things you hope to do. It's about living, not dying. Typical lists can range from simple items, like eating a slice of New York style pizza in New York, to once in a lifetime experiences, like setting a world record, and essentially everything in between. Goals can be extremely broad, like to fall in love, or extremely complex and specific, like to lose 20lbs and run a 10 km race in 55 minutes.

Bucket list items and goals can fall into many different types of categories such as life (fall in love), travel (see the Great Wall of China), experiences (meet Chuck Norris), health (lose 15 pounds), finance (pay off student debt), material (own a house), spiritual (read the Bible), seasonal (my summer bucket list), and a lot more. That is the beauty of a bucket list; it's never limited, and it should always keep growing and expanding with you through the ages, whether you're the former president of the United States of America, or a 24-year-old university graduate trying to make a mark on the world.

It may appear to simply boil down to a list of to do's before you die, but it's evolved into a guiding force to living and a roadmap of your success. Plus, keeping track of your achievements is a fantastic keepsake to share with family and friends for years to come.

Why you *need* a bucket list

Well, you might be thinking, "I know what I want to do in life, do I *really* need a bucket list?" YES. YES. YES! A bucket list should be written down and looked at on a regular basis. I don't know about you, but the amount of things that go through my head in a day would make any sane person's head spin. Writing things down helps me keep track and organize
my daily life, but also for my long-term goals. Undoubtedly, you jot down reminders for yourself to pick up milk, or finish the report by Friday. Bucket lists are kind of like a reminder for your life. Writing your goals and dreams down is the first step in figuring things out, to get things done. It's not just us at Bucketlist who think so; science is even on our side:

> Studies show that people who write down their goals, and share them with friends to be more accountable are over **33% MORE** successful than people that just write them down.[3]

This might make you cringe, but it all comes down to goal setting. Goal setting is an incredible tool in building your own success. The reason I feel setting goals through the bucket list mentality is a critical part of your daily life is threefold: direction, focus and purpose.

Direction

The process of creating a bucket list should be incredibly fun, but it can also be an incredibly insightful exercise. Is your bucket list primarily made of achieving financial goals, like that next big promotion or buying your first house? Or is it about discovering that exotic location in the middle of the Pacific Ocean? If the latter is the case, you may begin to realize that you highly value adventurous experiences over the traditional path. You'd be amazed at what you begin to uncover about yourself when you take the time to write out your hopes and ambitions. It's the first step on deciding what life you want to live and what sacrifices you might have to make in order to live them.

Focus

Did you know that the average person now consumes 12 hours of media, checks their phone 110 times a day and sees an estimated 5,000 marketing messages each day[4]? That is a lot of information to consume and concentrate on. It really is no wonder why so many people have trouble concentrating on what is truly and deeply important. A bucket list can be used as a tool to help bring clarity to what you really want to

---

[3] http://www.dominican.edu/dominicannews/study-backs-up-strategies-for-achieving-goals

[4] https://blog.percolate.com/2014/09/how-to-win-anyones-attention/?utm_content=bufferb4fa1&utm_medium=social&utm_source=twitter.com&utm_campaign=buffer

do in your life, and help influence your everyday activities to get you where you want to be. When I finally invested in the direction of my future, I discovered great clarity in my life ambitions. I began to put more thought and attention into everything I did. A major achievement of mine, this past year, was moving into the city center of Vancouver, Canada, one of the most expensive cities in North America. I wanted to achieve financial independence and stability for myself, and once I realized how important it was, I began to reevaluate a lot of my spending habits.

Purpose

Finally, a bucket list can be a guiding force in giving your life a deeper meaning. For a few months after I graduated university, I felt lost. What did I want to do with my life? My friends seemed to be finding adulthood, and I was about to move back into my parents' house while I figured things out. A bucket list's very essence is to map out your hopes and aspirations in life. If routine makes you feel like you're in a rut, having your goals at the forefront of your mind is a great motivator to get things done. It's a fantastic reminder of the bigger picture and not to get bogged down by everyday stress.

The Basics of Goal Setting

Mistakes are proof that you are trying.

When it boils down to it, bucket lists are essentially the first steps in proper goal setting. They help turn your dreams into goals into realities. Most people know what goal setting is, but why is it that not a lot of people succeed in their goals? Why is it that some people are more successful? How do some people seem to have it all? Well, my friends, it most likely boils down to goal setting and the power it holds. Does the word goal setting send chills down your spin, and not in a good way? Your grade school teacher probably drilled the importance of goal setting into your brain, but like most things in elementary school, it probably went in one ear, and out the other. Do you remember them asking, what do you want to do in your life, what do you want to achieve, or even where do you want to go to university? When you're 10 years old, these questions are daunting at best. So, inevitably, goal setting got - *and still has* - a pretty bad rap. I don't blame you. It was boring, repetitive, and sometimes even sad when failure hit you square in the face. But hear me out. Goal setting can be one of the most powerful tools to direct and propel you to have the best life possible.

In fact, science is here to back me up once again, with the famous – *and slightly infamous* – Harvard Masters of Business School Graduates study.

> *The 1979 Harvard MBA program.* In that year, the students were asked, "Have you set clear, written goals for your future and made plans to accomplish them?" Only three percent of the graduates had written goals and plans; 13 percent had goals, but they were not in writing; and a whopping 84 percent had no specific goals at all.
>
> Ten years later, the members of the class were interviewed again, and the findings, while somewhat predictable, were nonetheless astonishing. The 13 percent of the class who had goals were earning, on average, twice as much as the 84 percent who had no goals at all. And what about the three percent who had clear, written goals? They were earning, on average, ten times as much as the other 97 percent put together. [5]

Those are some huge numbers. To put things in perspective, the average starting salary for graduates in 1979 was a whopping 115k with a 20k signing bonus[6]. Even in today's standards that is quite an exceptionally 'comfortable' salary. With some simple math, and disregarding regular salary increases in the 10 years, the 3% graduate range who set clear written goals, were earning over 1 million dollars (10 times more) a year in 1989.

---

[5] McCormack, Mark H. *What They Don't Teach You at Harvard Business School.* Toronto: Bantam, 1984. Print.
[6] http://www.hbs.edu/about/facts-and-figures/Pages/mba-statistics.aspx

Goal setting is a powerful tool every individual on earth has the power of tapping in to. The process of setting goals starts with a little planning and as always a *lot* of work and dedication.

The task now is to figure out a smooth process to turn a vision into a reality, like the 3% of the 1979 graduate class of Harvard's Business School. Nothing's perfect, but with some exceptional coaching from the founders of Bucketlist – shout out to Bart and Jason – and a *lot* of reading and research, I can confidently say that understanding and setting SMART goals on a solid foundation of core values is a tried and tested way of achieving your dreams, one actionable step at a time. It's not an easy process, but it is worthwhile.

Core Values

But before I go too far ahead, let's start with core values, i.e. the foundation of any smart person's SMART goal. Values is another cliché, cringe-worthy word, right? Well, sort of. The word 'value' is just misunderstood these days. At the root of it, a value is defined as,

> *A person's principles or standards of behavior; one's judgment of what is important in life.*[7]

Simplified, values and especially core values are your backbone, what drives you to do what you do to find your flow in life, your true happiness. What does goal setting have to do with core values? Figuring out your core values helps align your goals with things you're truly passionate about, rather than goals that may be trendy or fashionable at the

---

[7] http://dictionary.reference.com/browse/value

time. A fantastic blog called *Early to Rise* has developed a pretty eye-opening and effective way of discovering your core values. Essentially, the author suggests we all start at the end, your funeral. What would be said about you if everyone you've figuratively touched in the world had the opportunity to speak openly and honestly about you? Put yourself in the shoes of your colleagues, your family, your friends, your neighbors and even your enemies.

Dig deep and try to be as honest as you can be, even if you might not like what they have to say.

> Imagine everything the people at your funeral could truthfully say about you — and then think about the way their words make you feel. If you don't feel good, it means that — in those relationships, at least — you are not living your life according to your core values. Now, for every negative statement you just imagined, ask yourself, "What would I like this person to be saying about me?" The answer to that question will reveal one of your core values.
>
> Let's say you imagined someone saying, "He was always struggling to make ends meet."
>
> That statement would make you feel bad, right? So then you imagine what you would like that person to say about you. You might come up with, "He struggled for a while, and then everything changed. He became very successful and died a wealthy man." If that statement makes you feel good, it's reasonable to say that acquiring wealth is a core value for you. And you would write it down like this: "I believe that financial success is a valuable and admirable accomplishment."

14

Negative Statement: "He was always struggling to make ends meet."

Positive Statement: "He struggled for a while, and then everything changed. He became very successful and died a wealthy man."

Core Value: "I believe that **financial success** is a valuable and admirable accomplishment.[8]"

Financial success is an example of a core value. Try to narrow down 5 or 6 of these core values that hold up your life. It's a challenging exercise, but a rewarding one in constructing a bucket list. Some of my core values are family, compassion, travel, and financial independence, and by situating my goals around these values, I've noticed I've become drawn to achieving these ambitions.

SMART Goal Setting

Now that your core values are solidified, or at least the theory behind them is, it's time to build upon them through a method of goal setting called SMART goal setting. Essentially, by developing your bucket list through SMART goals, your bucket list no longer becomes an unattainable entity. Instead, it is a remarkable roadmap to living life. What is a SMART goal, you may be asking? Well, a SMART goal stands for **Specific, Measurable, Attainable, Relevant, and Timely**. This is a method often used by the highest of achievers to set and break down lofty goals into doable steps. The beauty of following this framework is that you are

---

[8] http://www.earlytorise.com/how-to-find-your-core-values/#

15

much more likely to succeed in your goals than an unfocused and unaligned goal. Through the next few pages, we'll dive into the importance of each letter (S, M, A, R & T).

Although in a lot of businesses the principles of SMART goals are engrained in the everyday activities, for the average person it can seem kind of a daunting task. But even if you only break down a few of your big, hairy, audacious bucket list goals, you will have created a solid foundation for success in your life.

Let's Get to the Point - Specific Goals

Precision. The more accurate you are, the better, whether in sport or in business, hitting the nail on the head is always a good thing. How do you achieve precision? Details and thought. I don't want to turn the construction of your bucket list into a chore, but when writing out your bucket list, taking that extra step when writing each goal will make each item on your bucket list overwhelmingly easier to perceive and ultimately achieve. We, as a society, have to start putting the same thought and consideration into life goals as we would in business or in school. Personal development is just as important to society and ultimately we will create a happier, healthier community.

How many of you out there set New Year resolutions? A whole lot, I'm guessing. In fact, almost 70% of Canadians made resolutions in 2012! Astonishingly LESS than 24 hours later, nearly 20% broke their resolution.[9] These goals are

---

9

http://www.thestar.com/news/world/2013/01/01/new_yea rs_resolutions_by_the_numbers.html often too broad and general to have any real effect on your life.

What comes to your mind when you think of resolutions? I'll bet my left arm at least 90% of you thought of weight loss: "I want to lose weight in 2015!" Sound familiar? Well, let's break down this doozey of a goal into a more specific one.

Making Specific Goals
So how can we turn losing weight into a more precise goal? A simple method to setting a specific goal is by answering these 5 W's.

> What: What do I want to accomplish? – *Lose 10 pounds*
> Why: The purpose of accomplishing the goal. – *Feel healthier*
> Who: Who is involved? – *Myself and my best friend*
> Where: Identify the location. – *Gym at 7:30am*
> When: When do you want to achieve this by? *February 27, 2015*

The more information, the better, but even just by answering the first question, you've already developed a more solid and in-depth goal than just 'losing weight.' When you lay out the guidelines for your goal, taking the next step is much easier to achieve. Before you know it, just from making your goal specific, you will begin to subconsciously work toward it through your everyday decisions and choices.

Measurable Goals

Let's look at the 'm' in SMART goals. In this case, M stands for measurable. Adding the M to your goals is a great way to keep you on track to checking off your bucket list. Although bucket lists are a great place to track what you hope to achieve in your entire lifetime, they're also a fantastic place to map out some yearly accomplishments you hope to achieve.

The simplest ways to make sure your goals are measurable is to set an overall due date, and to create targets to hit along the way. A goal without a target date is just a dream, which is fine for some of the items of your bucket list. But if you're ready to commit to *actually* achieving these goals, measurable targets will create the urgency and commitment needed to succeed. Essentially, it will transform your dreams into tangible goals.

How to Set Measurable Targets

Start by setting a completion date. This is probably one of the hardest steps because some of the items on your bucket list are big, hairy, overly ambitious goals that we just don't really know when we'll be able to check off, and that's okay. But for your SMART goals – ones you hope to achieve in the next couple of years – having a completion date is like lighting the light at the end of the tunnel. You begin to visualize completing it and create a sense of urgency and excitement to get going on your bucket list dreams.

Secondly, pick out some key milestones to hit along the way. For example, I plan on running the Vancouver Sun Run (a 10km race) at the end of April. So my halfway goal is to be able to run 8 km in under an hour, which for me is realistic because if I'm completely honest with you, running isn't my favorite thing to do. When I first began training, I set out to run the ten minute mile, a fitness test I remembered from my days as a high school soccer player. It isn't the most difficult of goals, but like I said before, I'm not a runner. So once I strapped on my sneakers for a few days, I decided it was time to tackle the ten minute mile. It may have been 10 minutes and 45 seconds, but hitting the mile in under eleven minutes gave me a weird sense of accomplishments that helped motivate me to keep training. I still have a long way to go, but the little wins are getting me very excited to hit the big goal on April 19th.

Attainable Goals

I've always wanted to be legitimate royalty - too many Disney movies growing up - but sadly at my age I've realized I don't think Prince Harry is going to turn around and propose to me - *at least not for a little while.*

The same can be said for setting SMART goals and making them **attainable**. Understanding our limitations doesn't mean we have to settle for the mundane. I think it means the opposite. It means we can set our sights on outrageously awesome goals that, with some work and planning, we can *actually* achieve. And let me tell you, accomplishing these types of goals is so, so sweet!

In order for your goal to be realistic, it must be a goal, which you are willing and able to work toward. We all hope to wake up a multimillionaire, but I've come to terms that I don't think that's going to happen. Setting goals that are achievable (in this lifetime) will help you to keep on track with accomplishing your goal because you won't feel like it is completely beyond your reach.

Relevant Goals

The next step in developing some SMART bucket list goals is to make your bucket list relevant to your life and core values. It's so important to choose goals that matter because you begin to attach emotional meaning to them, sometimes even just subconsciously. Ask yourself, does this seem worthwhile? Will achieving this bucket list goal be something I'm proud to share for the rest of my life? If you answered yes, likely your goals will hold a higher meaning to yourself, providing you with more driving motivation to succeed.

Time-Bound Goals

The last leg of the SMART goal process is setting timely goals. When you have a task to do, but no deadline, how long do you take to do it? Of course it depends on what you're tasked to do, but chances are it will take a lot longer than expected (or than it should) to complete. In fact, some studies show that giving yourself micro-deadlines or targets, will help beat the dreaded procrastination[10]. The same mentality can be translated to your bucket list goals.

Have timely goals by figuring out the realistic time it should take to achieve them. Little milestones are a great way to stay motivated and keep your goals at the forefront of your mind. Let's break down an example of how you can add a timely goal to a popular bucket list goal.

Running a Marathon
Running a marathon is a great item to have on your bucket list. Not only is it physically challenging, but it also requires months of dedication, training and focus in order to achieve it.

---

[10] https://www.princeton.edu/mcgraw/library/for-students/avoiding-procrastination/

To make running a marathon a timely goal, start by choosing a marathon you want to run. Obviously, your physical shape and endurance determines how far away it should be for training, but let's say a year is generally a good place to start.

By setting an end time, you've taken a huge leap to making your bucket list item of running a marathon happen. Essentially, you've created a sense of urgency for your dream. The second major step is identifying milestones along the way, like running 10 miles without stopping or training four days a week for a month. Targets are also additionally helpful for your bucket list goals because they are the ultimate excuses to celebrate your "mini-wins." After all, your bucket list is all about living life to the fullest, so obviously it should be really fun!

Now that we've covered some of the best steps you can take to set SMART goals, it's time to dive into your bucket list – let's start crushing it.

Failure as Part of Success

Of course, I would be wrong if I didn't talk about failure at this point of the book. It is inevitable, and it sucks, but it's not the end of the world. Sometimes there are bumps in the road, but it's important to embrace them as learning experiences and progress. Michelle Barber so eloquently discusses this journey in a recent post titled, "Failure as Part of the Bucket List Experience." Read about her experience below.

> Are some of your bucket list goals pretty wild? Way outside your comfort zone, not to mention your budget, skill or ability zones? And are you afraid you

may try and fail at some of these goals? Then you and I have some things in common.

My bucket list is the To Do list of an adventurous, athletic, wealthy genius. I love who I see when I look at that list: Michelle on top of mountains and racing cars, learning languages and living like an expat, owning a radio station and fighting with nunchucks. And I've tried to live up to this person. Oh, how I've tried. I have also fallen short on several occasions.

- For years, I had a bucket list that gathered dust because I was *deep* in debt.
- Once I got out of debt, I went on my first beach vacation and ended up watching too much TV, with the beach on one side of my rental and a bike path on the other.
- Last year, I attempted to bicycle around Vermont using Adventure Cycling Association maps. I biked for two days and called it quits on a painfully long and steep hill.
- This year, I went out on the Long Trail, a 272 mile path along Vermont's Green Mountains. I made it 60+ miles battling bum shoes, broken tent poles, a too-heavy pack, and physical activity beyond my ability.

Amidst all these "failures" – this is where I start using quotes around that word – I learned a lot of lessons.

Listen to the way you frame failure
What does the voice in your head say? "I'm a failure, a loser, a quitter." "I can't do this." "I'm just not good

enough or fit enough or I don't have the money or the willpower." Articulate the voice so it's not insidious.

Reframe failure so you can move forward
If the thought is "I can't afford this," move that to "I am saving up money to make this happen." If you feel like a quitter, give yourself credit for dreaming, for starting. This is where you write your own story. Don't make yourself the bad guy! Flip every negative comment into a positive or constructive assessment.

Constructively assess the failure
Take stock, write down the things you learned. Make a list of the tactical lessons, as well as what you learned about yourself.

Failure Moving Forward

Maybe your bucket list was the brainchild of a younger self and it no longer fits. Maybe, by learning what you don't enjoy, you've freed up resources for things you know you enjoy. Or maybe it's time to change everything after this "failure" because the person your bucket list reflects is the person you want to be.

It's true: I haven't completed the Long Trail – yet. But I know what I need to do for next summer. And the bike trip will happen another time. I've also conquered my debt and am living a life I love, even if it sometimes means watching too much TV on a beach holiday.

There aren't too many "failures" when it comes to your bucket list. There are (figurative or literal) bumps, bruises, scrapes, lateral moves, and lessons learned.

But if you see that as part of the fun, your bucket list will teach you lessons for the rest of your life.

Persistence

Accept it, failing is going to happen. Let it happen, pick yourself on and move on. If everyone on this planet was scared to fail, progression would be impossible. It doesn't matter how smart, or privileged you are, every single person on this earth has failed at one point or another. So why are we all so hung up on it? What you should focus on is what happens after failure. After you fall down, and get up, what do you do? Do you reevaluate your mistake, and approach your obstacle from another perspective? Persist.

"The most interesting thing about a postage stamp is the persistence with which it sticks to its job." – Napoleon Hill

PART 2

Decide What You Want To Do
And Do it

"There are two types of people who will tell you that you cannot make a difference in this world: those who are afraid to try and those who are afraid you will succeed."

- Ray Goforth

CREATING YOUR ULTIMATE BUCKET LIST

Mapping Your Future, Mapping Your Life

Breaking down over 220,000 real bucket lists, I've noticed that a lot of these lists have similar themes and directions in common. From travel, to learning a new skill, to extreme sports, everyone wants to live a thrilling, fulfilled and adventurous life. Bucket lists are as unique as the person writing them, and hold specific meaning to each person. Interestingly enough, some overarching themes started to emerge.

Let's dive into the top 5 most popular categories of bucket list goals to look into what makes these types of bucket list ideas so appealing to so many different types of people. Not only that, but in the coming pages, I hope to share with you some of the *real* steps you need to take to start turning these bucket list longings into realities and then into memories.

As we said in the introduction, the beauty of a bucket list is that it is really up to you what you value to be on your life list. As long as it's something you love doing and something that will make you happy, go ahead and add it to your bucket list. In fact, some of our super-star bucket list makers have over 9,000 – yes, 9,000 – bucket list goals! And a popular response when asked why is because one of their top bucket list goals is to never stop adding to their bucket list.

So let's dive in to the big kahuna of the bucket list world - travel.

TRAVEL

*"We travel not to escape life,
but for life not to escape us."*
- Anonymous

Since the dawn of modern transportation, travel has swept the hearts and minds of people all over the world to experience new sights, sounds and places; to talk to individuals in different languages; to taste the spices and delicacies only available in the remote villages of Southeast Asia. Travel takes hold of the realists and the dreamers of the world, and has even inspired the insurgence of the German word 'wanderlust,' a.k.a. the strong desire to travel.

So let me ask you, if money were no issue, where would you go? Would you hit up the wonders of the world? Or hike deep into the jungles of western Africa? Would you jump in the car and drive to the nearest ocean, or hop on the next flight across the world? When you travel, your imagination is your only limitation – well, and your budget. But every penny spent is worth it; travel is truly the ultimate bucket list goal. It broadens your mind, opens you up to different parts of the globe, and allows you to soak in the awe-astounding sites that figuratively and literally take your breath away.

In the next section of this book, we'll really dive into how you can begin to accomplish all your travel related bucket list goals, since it can be one of the more challenging and expensive goals on a list. I'll get into the nitty-gritties of how you can save up, and plan the best trip ever, as well as how you can get ready to transform from a tourist to a traveler.

Why are travel goals so popular?

Travel is important because it fundamentally transforms us all. It's my opinion that experiencing countries and cultures makes humanity better; we develop a deeper understanding of each other, and begin to appreciate the difference more and more with each adventure. It's a badge of honor all true travelers wear with pride, to share their stories and experiences from their journeys. Ask any traveler about a country or city and prepare to be bombarded with stories, tips and tricks. Watch them light up recounting these stories, and see the pure joy transform their persona.

The beauty of goals relating to travel is they provide infinite opportunities to achieve and succeed with bucket list ideas that are otherwise not possible. The ability to explore and discover is experienced by far too few people. With a monster of a category like travel, a few subsections emerge.

Destinations
Of course, the underlining objective to travel is to experience new places, like cities, countries or even continents. Venice, Bora Bora, New York City, Tokyo, and Paris come out as some of the top places people want to visit. Images of these beautiful places often circulate around Tumblr and Pinterest

Boards, but nothing compares to stepping out on the top platform of the Eiffel tower. Looking over the breathtakingly gorgeous city is indescribable, and if you're lucky like me, you might even be treated to witnessing an incredible proposal.

If you're short on funds, take a look at all the local towns and cities that surround you. I grew up in a fairly small city, Regina, Saskatchewan, Canada. Many people I grew up with had never even seen the ocean, never mind venturing to the opposite side of the world. Growing up in Regina, I probably didn't appreciate the adventures that waited locally and regionally, but looking back, the small towns surrounding the city were truly diamonds waiting to be discovered. For example, did you know that Moose Jaw, Saskatchewan, infamously housed gangster Al Capone, who had an underground bootleg headquarters? Literally his operations were underground in the now pseudo-famous "Tunnels of Moose Jaw." Believe it or not, once-in-a-lifetime and memorable experiences are sometimes just a short car ride away.

Culture
Probably one of my favorite reasons to travel is to experience the multitude of cultures prevalent in this big old globe of ours. Take Spain, a beautiful country with so much culture it's ridiculous and sometimes *very* surprising. When I was in Barcelona in summer 2010, the festival called the Eve of Sant Joan literally took me by surprise when I woke up to what I assumed was an explosion (I watch too much CNN). Turns out, this festival celebrates Sant Joan and the midsummer on June 23rd with fireworks all day until dawn the next day. It's hard to ignore the festival when the sights and sounds surround you everywhere you go. Barcelona went out with a BANG.

But culture often exposes itself in everyday and seemingly routine activities when you are abroad. Take much of Spain and Italy; the afternoon siesta is just a part of life. And it may seem unusual to close down shops and businesses to take an afternoon snooze, but it is engrained in the identities of these countries, and in my opinion it's utterly brilliant. Who doesn't like a good afternoon nap?

Being in tune with the cultural norms of the city/country you're visiting is a practice travelers should take up. There's no point being upset that the cafés are closed during the high sun hours. Instead, take that time to head back to your hotel or hostel, rest up and re-energize for the evening to come. Anyway, the night is when the fun really starts, so you better be rested and ready to dance the night away.

Food
Okay, my first favorite reason to travel may be all the yummy food. And this is a goal that can easily be adapted to your local city, heck even your local neighborhood. Of course, there isn't anything quite like having a big bowl of aribiata spaghetti from the kitchens of a true Italian Mama in Rome, but you'd be surprised of the local cuisine that's available in neighborhoods across your city. Here in Vancouver, you can travel from China to little Italy in the course of a 20-minute train ride.

But let's get back to all the food you're going to experience on your travels. The one rule you really just *have* to follow is try everything at least once. Some things are going to be gross, have weird textures and smell pretty awful, but sometimes gems emerge, and you might even find your new favorite. Have you ever tried pigeon? Yes, the rats of the sky! I'm not saying it's something I'll have every day or catch and cook for myself *ever*, but to be completely honest it tastes like chicken. Insects are another surprising delicacy discovery. Again, I will never eat an insect I see in the wild or in my bathroom tub, but in the markets of places like Uganda, I'm told they are readily available, and quite frankly are similar to a potato chip: deep fried, crunchy and salty. Plus, did you know that bugs have some of the highest protein content available? They are a great source of nutrition if you are ever stranded on a desert island – FYI.

People

What would travelling be without all the incredible people? Not very fun at all. If you are traveling alone, you have a fantastic opportunity to make friends around the world. If you're an independent traveler – and I hope at least once in your life you travel alone – traveling really forces you to come out of your shell, and open yourself up to the world around you. There are endless benefits to making these connections around the world. Free accommodation, to start, plus local tour guides, and you could even gain a pen pal – remember those? But on top of that, travelling alone, and I know this is going to sound awfully cliché, you really are able to find yourself and test what you're capable as a fierce human being.

Taking the leap and travelling alone may seem like a very scary and intimidating thing to do, but it really is a great way to be forced into opening yourself up to the world. I know that I often rely on the support I get from friends and family. Travelling independently forces you to rely on yourself. And this newfound confidence often translates to passing every language and cultural barrier, and attracting other likeminded, adventurous and amazing people.

Experiences

Finally, traveling is all about being exposed to experiences you wouldn't normally have the opportunity to achieve. Travelers know this too well; the experiences are worth every penny they cost. Although you can scuba dive virtually anywhere with a deep enough pool, diving the Great Barrier Reef with a loggerhead turtle by your side is a much more exotic and rewarding occurrence. There's something about the authenticity of having a once-in-a-lifetime experience in a surreal location that creates long-lasting and exhilarating memories.

I'm fortunate enough to have some pretty cool travel stories under my belt. I've always had an affinity for animals, so seeing them in the wild is amazing. When I went to Mauritius – a tiny island off the coast of Madagascar in the Indian Ocean – I never expected to be so immersed in a location that is similar to that of Jurassic Park, minus the Tyrannosaurus Rex. Mauritius is full of lush palm trees, beautiful cascading waterfalls and exotic wildlife that this prairie girl never expected to see. One of my favorite memories from the trip was seeing the monkeys in the wild. Although they seemed to be quite accustomed to humans, I was not accustomed to seeing them. They were almost statuesque perched on top of the railings overlooking a magnificent waterfall. On another outing to the white sandy beaches of Mauritius, I went for a stroll, but not just any standard walk along the beach; this was an underwater walk, where a giant bubble helmet was plopped on your head and connected to an air hose so you could breathe. You were able to complete a circuit under the sea, feeling what it must be like to be a mermaid/merman. The coolest part was having a tropical fish nibble on a piece of bread right out of my hand.

One of the biggest tips I can share with you is to open yourself up to unexpected 'incidences' – and to remember that sometimes sh*t happens. Sometimes no matter how much you try, things don't go the way they're planned. I've had so many wonderful trips that have gone off without a hitch, but there have been a couple of unforeseen disasters. A two-hour delay in Madrid due to a "mechanical error" once turned into a 3-day delay getting home. But on the bright side, our flight was put up in a beautiful hotel with food and beverages paid for. It was definitely something I will never forget.

As I hope you can see by now, travel is a beautiful, *beautiful* thing, with few limitations. However, what we hear all the time is that people feel they lack money, time and information in order for them to achieve their travel related bucket list goals. My biggest advice to you is to persist.

My last tip before the trip is to create your own destination bucket list. Planning out exactly what activities you want to do and attractions you want to see will help you get more done on your trip and less time wasted! Scotland is one of my favorite countries that I've visited. Take a look at a few of the activities to cross off your list in Scotland.

Scottish Bucket List

A Wee Bit about Scotland

Scotland is the birthplace of Brave Heart *and* the Loch Ness Monster. To many, that would be enough of a draw to go, but trust me there *really* is so much more. From rolling hills, to medieval architecture, and even to the best whiskey in the world, Scotland has so much to offer! The capital city Edinburgh is surrounded by priceless architecture, most notably the Edinburgh Castle perched on top of the hill overlooking the city.

The Scottish Bucket List

Take a sip of Lagavulin Whiskey in Islay, Scotland
If you're a *Parks and Rec* fan, you'll know about Lagavulin Whiskey, the drink of choice for Ron Swanson (i.e. the manliest man in the world). And maybe I've been watching too much *P&R*, but drinking a glass of whiskey from the source while breathing the highland air sounds wonderful to me.

Visit the Puffins
Puffin colonies take up residence along the coast of Scotland and spend their summers on the beach (sounds like a sweet vacation). If you want to catch a glimpse of these comical and ever so cute birds, check out the Isle of May (around May) and you'll almost be guaranteed to see a puffin in real life.

Take a tour of Edinburgh Castle
Located on castle rock, dominating the Edinburgh skyline, Edinburgh Castle is one of the most picturesque castles I have had the pleasure of visiting. With its sprawling views, the castle was a prominent feature in many of the battles of independence! Just one of the many fun facts you'll learn on the tours.

Spot Nessy in Loch Ness
No matter what anybody tells you, the Loch Ness Monster is real, and I have photographic evidence. The blurry dot in the middle of one of my photographs is the definitive proof! Don't believe me? Head there yourself; it is also one of the

most gorgeous views in nature if you're not lucky enough to spot Nessy for yourself!

Take a swig of Iron Brew
Did you know that Iron Brew was recently banned in Canada? I know, I'm outraged, too! The orange liquid of the gods doesn't actually contain any iron, but it is a bit of an acquired taste. Iron Brew and Scotland go hand in hand like apple pie and America.

Visit the William Wallace Memorial
William Wallace (aka Brave Heart) is the pride of Scotland, sacrificing life and limb for the great nation! The memorial located about an hour outside of Glasgow, houses the original sword of William Wallace and is about the size of a very tall human being. It's something spectacular to see.

Participate in a Burns Supper
The Burns Supper is a quintessential Scottish Activity. The supper includes an introduction of the traditional haggis by one of the smoothest instruments in the world... the bagpipes. Topped off with some poetry and whiskey, you'll be a resident Scot after attending one of these.

Hike one of Scotland's Great Trails
Moore walk (or hill walk) through some of the best trails in Britain. There are so many stunning natural sights to see along the way. And the best part is, you can take the family and tick off a bite-sized chunk of one of the routes by doing a bit each weekend or tackling the whole route in one go.

Experience a Scottish Ceilidh
A highland ceilidh refers to a party where you partake in traditional highland dancing to gaelic music, but really it is so

much more. The whole community gets involved and it's a chance to show off your best jig.

Attend the highland games
Finally, the highland games are globally renowned and take place during the summer months. Feats of strength? Check! Delicious food? Check! Dancing? Check! Really, what more could you ever want?

Kick start your travel micro-adventures by narrowing down some exciting activities you can do before you go.

What kind of book about bucket lists would this be without some inspiration for you to consider for your own bucket list?

Here are our top 10 places for you to add to your list.

1. Paris, France

2. Venice, Italy

3. Niagara Falls, Ontario

4. White House, Washington, DC

5. Sydney, Australia

6. Coliseum, Rome, Italy

7. Great Wall of China

8. New York, New York

9. Holland

10. Tokyo, Japan

LIVING THE EXTREME DREAM

"The purpose of life is to live it, to taste experience to the utmost, to reach out eagerly and without fear for newer and richer experience."
— *Eleanor Roosevelt*

One of the next most prominent bucket list goal categories falls under the extreme adrenaline seeking adventures. Think bungee jumping, skydiving, and generally anything a 14-year-old may yell YOLO at. This is something I struggle with. Just the thought of jumping out of a plane with nothing but a stranger and a backpack strapped to my back is utterly amazing and utterly terrifying at the same time – but mostly very, very terrifying.

But for the sake of a complete bucket list, let's dive into living an extreme life. Can I ask you another question? What makes your heart race and your palms sweat just thinking about it? Whatever the answer, it most likely would fit under this bucket list category.

The Science of the Extreme

Standing at the edge of a cliff, most people's reactions would be to run and hide, right? So, why is it that some people would have the audacity to jump? It seems to go against all the laws of Mother Nature, but there must be something to these activities to draw so many people to do them. Turns out it may go back to man's most basic instinct, fight or flight, caused by the production of adrenaline.

> "Adrenaline junkies keep moving up the ladder of excitement: zip lining, spelunking, bungee jumping, ballooning, scuba diving, mountain climbing, hang gliding, and the scariest one of all: public speaking. It's all about reaching that feeling we express as, "What a rush!" It feels empowering, and makes us feel that we can do anything. Unfortunately, the feeling is fleeting, but for the few moments it lingers we feel as if we're walking on air.[11]"

If you crave that feeling of danger, take a look at a few of my favorite reasons to have extreme adventures on your bucket list.

Adrenaline
Imagine the feeling of electricity coursing through your veins as you feel invincible after you defied death by jumping out of a plane. You feel so alive! Adrenaline goes back to your natural and most basic instincts, fight or flight, preparing your body and psyching up your mind for a potential predator or attack. Adrenaline is a hormone released by your body as a response to a stressful situation. Now that we no

---

[11] http://www.psychologytoday.com/blog/the-main-ingredient/201207/seeking-danger-find-sense-life

longer have to fight off the elements or one another for survival, adrenaline is a feeling humanity seeks. Scientists believe that's some of the most underlying reasons as to why we even have a yearning for extreme activities.

Just like the travel goals, the extreme fall into a few common and thrilling sub-categories.

Excitement

Some of our favorite bucket list activities would fall under this category: the obvious like bungee jumping, sky diving and cliff jumping, but getting a tattoo, or even throwing a dart and going to the place it lands on is, in my opinion, just as extreme and exciting. As the great Spice Girls once said, "Spice up your life," and excitement is surely the seasoning of the living. Of course, if you embody the bucket list ideals, excitement will be second nature to you. You might even laugh, where others like me would run away and hide.

People seek out and fall head over heels, passionately in love with the opportunity to excite. One of the most sought-after bucket list goals is to skydive. Skydiving, as you most likely know, is when you jump out of a plane, and float back down to earth. I have never done such an exciting adventure in my life, but I can understand the reasoning behind why someone might skydive. What it must be like to feel what it's like to fly.

Once you begin to push your limits, you can see how the yearning for excitement can grow. But is there a limit to pushing your limits? And if there is, what is it? Hopefully, my friends, for you there never will be one. And here's why! Take our friend Felix Baumgartner. You may not recognize the name, but I'm sure you've heard the story. Felix Baumgartner broke the world record for skydiving an estimated 39 kilometers[12]... pretty much from space! He sat in a helium balloon and rose to the outer ozone of the earth. Felix then took the ultimate leap, free falling through the sky before gracefully landing back on earth. This jump was thought to be near impossible before Felix pushed the barriers of possibility.

If you haven't heard of Felix or haven't seen the video, I highly recommend you watch it. Breaking your personal limits will set you free. All this talk of excitement perfectly leads into our next category, danger.

Danger
If you were on a highway to the danger zone, where would you go? The element of danger has always been a strong draw for extreme bucket list goals. As the saying goes, if everyone could do it, it would be easy. But you're not everyone; you laugh in the face of danger. So what makes the element of danger so appealing? Adding risk to your bucket list is literally like staring death in the eye, coming out the other side stronger than ever, and thriving to tell the tale.

Think about events such as running with the bulls. The event originated when the bulls needed transport from their holding pen to the arena where the bull fights would occur. Originally, young men who wanted to show off their fearlessness and bravado would jump in with the bulls[13]. Danger and adrenaline seekers go hand-in-hand, but hopefully the riskier bucket list goals are in a controlled and calculated environment.

Once-in-a-lifetime

---

[12] http://en.wikipedia.org/wiki/Felix_Baumgartner
[13] http://en.wikipedia.org/wiki/Running_of_the_Bulls

Finally, the extreme bucket list goals are extreme because many of them are once-in-a-lifetime opportunities. These kinds of bucket list activities will always be remembered for the rest of your lifeand transform into the best and lasting memories.

If you're like me, slightly averse to putting your life in complete and utter danger, why not ease into the extreme lifestyle with a little paragliding.

Paraglide

It takes a certain kind of spirit to willingly jump off of a mountain. Not just jump, but run full speed at what should be impending doom. Yet instead of plummeting to the rocks below, you take flight and gracefully glide through the air, getting a perspective on the world previously reserved only for birds.

Paragliding is an experience unlike any other, embracing both the daredevil and poet that live inside each and every one of us. Here's why paragliding needs to go on your bucket list:

Hike and Enjoy Nature
This may be obvious, but in order to reach these summits (to jump from) you often have to hike up with your equipment. I'm not going to lie, it will be a grind, but what could be a greater way to get down the mountain (other than sledding) than to literally fly down the face of the hill!

Conquer a Fear
Paragliding is a great medium extreme sport for people just getting a taste for adrenaline! It's not quite as scary as jumping out of an airplane, but it's still going to get your heart pumping. An added bonus is having an expert guide to

all of the grunt work for you. All you need to do is sit back in the harness, trust that everything is going to be okay, and enjoy the once-in-a-lifetime experience that will make a lot of your friends jealous.

You're Flying

There are few times in life when you can truly feel like you're flying free. The first is when you reach that pivotal moment on the swings in grade school, and you were certain that you might never come back down. A second time may be if you are brave enough to take the leap out of an airplane. The third, and a solid medium between the former two, is paragliding.

Extreme bucket list goals are the type of adventures where you're too busy having the time of your life to care about much else. They give you that natural 'high' and stories to last you a lifetime. If you're a little more risk adverse, there are still a lot of activities you can try to get that adrenaline high without risking your life. One of the best moments for me was when I learned to surf in Tofino, BC, Canada.

For those of you that don't know, Tofino is located in the Pacific North West. It's not polar vortex cold, but it ain't no tropical beach. It was chilly, but we were excited, so we suited up, carried our boards out to the beach and prepared to be the next Kelly Slater in no time. There was one slight problem: the extent of our training was (and I quote) just paddle, paddle, paddle, and when you feel it, just up throw a shaka and ride it out. We rented our gear from an awesome local surf shop called Relec Surf Shop in Ucluelet (they are seriously the best) and set off to crush one of my top bucket list items.

Not the greatest instructions, but I had watched *Blue Crush* enough times to know what I was doing. Except, no, I didn't. The best way I can describe how my muscles felt the next day was (excuse my language) it felt like getting bitch slapped by Mother Nature. The ocean deserves our utmost respect.

But aside from that, the feeling when you finally figure out how to ride a wave (kind of) is incredible! What made this weekend truly memorable was achieving something that I'd wanted to do for so long with some of my closest friends.

Looking to add a little excitement to your bucket list? Check out the top 10 extreme bucket list goals below.

Top 10 Extreme Bucket List Goals

1. Ride in a Hot Air Balloon

2. Bungee Jump

3. Go Rock Climbing

4. Experience Zero Gravity

5. Get a Tattoo

6. Travel by Helicopter

7. Skydive

8. Flyboard

9. Paraglide

10. Surf the Big Swell

PERSONAL DEVELOPMENT

"If you are not willing to learn, no one can help you.
If you are determined to learn, no one can stop you."
- *Anonymous*

Every January 1, millions of people set goals they want to achieve in the upcoming year. Things are bright, fresh and full of possibilities! Resolutions are great, right? But by February 15th, I'm guessing 90% of people have, sadly, given up and slipped into their old – bad – habits. Personal development should be something we strive for on a daily basis. Yet sometimes this category is grossly abused. What could be better than learning and growing as a human being? The flashy and exciting goals like traveling or the adrenaline-fueled adventures often outshine skills and development. But new skills are some of the most valuable goals you can accomplish on your bucket list. They not only help you with your personal development, but also have such a positive impact on the world around you.

Realistically, just 8% of people keep with their pledges. Resolutions get a bad rap because they are set with the wrong state of mind. We see that people often set these goals on a faulty foundation of what is popular. The Paleo diet? Sounds like a great way to drop the pounds. Juice cleanse? Time to detox the skin and your stomach. But once a difficult patch hits, it's easier to give up than to readjust your goal.

The underlining reason we see so many goals fail is because there is a lack of effort in the planning stage of goal setting. Especially with these goals, it's important to follow some of the goal setting tips we went over in the first section of the book. And always keep your motivation at the forefront of your mind to help you keep on track to success.

It's a weird thing when you step back and think about what drives you as a person to do what you want to do. I'm not just talking about working or even working out, but the little everyday activities. Use this source of influence and motivation to create habits in your daily life. If you wake up just 30 mins earlier every morning to work out, but add 5 years of quality time spent with your loved ones, isn't that worth it? Start putting these little actions into perspective with the big picture. You begin to live with a sense of purpose.

Not only do these types of goals help develop your personal life, but they also can relate to your career, your family and anything you touch. As we see from the high failure rate of resolutions, sometimes these types of goals can be the most challenging to achieve. There is little accountability to other people, and ultimately if you fail, you're only letting yourself down. This has to change! Toward the end of this chapter, we'll dive into proven strategies to help make your personal development goals stick now, and for months to come.

Why is Personal Development even a Bucket List Category?

We see these types of goals so often because human beings, and especially the outstanding bucket list go-getting human beings, want to be the best possible version of themselves they can be. The thought of mastering a skill or conquering a challenge probably excites you. Well, you're not alone; did you know that nearly 50% of Americans set New Year resolutions for themselves? At the beginning of the year, anything seems possible to achieve – you just need a little hard work and determination.

Below are some of the most popular subcategories of personal development.

New Skills
Let's start with the basics, new skills. It takes 10,000 hours to master any one skill. From learning a new language, to fencing, you have to put in the time to reap the rewards. We see more and more people adding these goals to their bucket lists on a daily basis. Sadly, time and again, we hear that these are some of the most difficult goals to accomplish. What do you do when you set out to learn a new skill? I usually find myself completely obsessed to master the skill, at first. But after a while, I get bored, frustrated, or just forget, and once an obstacle arises, ultimately I give up. To get over this happening to you, we know that breaking down your goals into smaller, but detailed steps create habits. Habits, as I'm sure you know, are *much more* difficult to break, and once they are engrained in your routine, you'll be picking up new skills in no time!

A very common bucket list goal is learning a second language. It is a challenging goal at the best of times. If you're thinking of picking up a second or third language, here are a few tips for completing this bucket list goal.

Learning a New Language

Learning a new language is a popular bucket list goal because it's challenging, it's interesting, and it's a lifelong skill that can improve your travel and your life. But because it's difficult, not many people succeed in the way they wish. While there are countless ways to learn a language, here are a few tips if you're just getting started and need a little nudge.

Set Targets

Like all bucket list goals, you need to make realistic deadlines to track your progress and be able to strive for your future success. You can set long term goals, like when you'll have full conversations in the language, and progress markers like when you'll have simple conversations, when you'll be able to introduce yourself, and when you can grasp what is being said in a short dialogue. These are up to you; just make sure you're pushing yourself, but allow for time if things get difficult.

Collect Resources

You'll obviously need resources to learn the language, like a translation dictionary, audio files, and books. It's also a good idea to get movies (from that country, not dubbed) and watch them both for the language and for cultural references or idioms.

Use It

Memorizing vocabulary and listening to the language isn't enough to get you speaking and communicating. It's important to practice forming words and sentences that are unfamiliar to our English mouths and to quickly listen and understand the foreign words. You can find a language exchange partner online or look in your community for classes or language groups to speed up your progress.

Stay Positive

Learning a foreign language is tough. If it weren't, everyone would speak every language. But just remember why you want to learn that language; maybe it's for an upcoming trip or you want to communicate with people you know in their language. Whatever the case, keep reminding yourself, that way you keep from feeling down if things are moving slower than you'd hoped.

Immerse as much as possible

If you're learning a language for a trip, the trip might just put the finishing touches on your language learning. Try to speak as little English as possible so you immediately immerse yourself into the rhythm and mindset of the new language. If you don't have plans to travel, maybe plan a trip! Or, if you can't, try to block off days, or even a few hours, where you won't hear any English and will try to keep English off of your mind. Listen to the language, read, and if possible, talk to others.

Other types of Personal Development Bucket List Goals

Health and Fitness

Goals revolving around fitness are a constant addition to many people's bucket lists. Like most types of personal development bucket list goals, they are challenging, and take dedication, but when you achieve them, you always emerge a better and *literally* stronger person. Those who are successful in fitness goals often work toward an ultimate challenge, like a marathon, climbing a mountain, or even completing an

Ironman. These goals, just like learning a new skill, often rely on you breaking them down into daily steps.

When you hear of the sheer distances in a single Ironman Triathlon, it would make a normal person quiver in fear.

- 2.4-mile (3.86 km) swim
- 112-mile (180.25 km) bicycle ride
- 26.2-mile (42.2 km) run[14]

Determination is an understatement. Athletes who compete in these races incorporate training into everything they do because they know the payoff when they cross the finish line is greater than anything they had to sacrifice.

A key initiative to take when making your health and fitness goals a reality is to turn your actionable steps into daily habits. A lot of persistence and determination is involved to create these habits, but as soon as it becomes a part of your routine, you'll be achieving your fitness dreams in no time.

Career
When you spend the majority of your week at work, isn't it important to set goals to control the direction in which you want to go? Whether you want to climb the corporate ladder, become a doctor or travel abroad to work in the non-profit industry, having a clear end goal in mind will help you progress smoothly and efficiently. For your career, lay out a few objectives you'd like to hit. Salary goals, lifestyle balance, and position are a few things to consider when applying for a job. Conversely, evaluating what you want in your life will give you perspective on a career path to take. Starting a business might be the right path for you. Goal setting is so important in business. It gives you vision for the future and allows you to take action toward your goals. Take perhaps

---

[14] http://en.wikipedia.org/wiki/Ironman_Triathlon

the most infamous entrepreneur there is, Sir Richard Branson.

> *"I believe in goals. It's never a bad thing to have a dream, but I'm practical about it. I don't sit daydreaming about things that are impossible. I set goals and then work out how to achieve them. Anything I want to do in life I want to do well and not half-heartedly."*
> *- Sir Richard Branson*

When setting career goals and objectives, having a mentor or the advice from a trusted colleague is key to taking the right initiatives. It's no secret that I believe in the power of having a mentor. Someone to model your behavior and career on, who can help advise your decisions, and someone who is there for your best interest, is an extremely fortunate position to be in. But sadly, so many people are left to navigate life, with little or no guidance. Having a role model, or a mentor can be the catalyst for your life.

Having a Mentor

A mentor is simply an experienced or trusted adviser. But what makes having a mentor exceptional is the one on one connection and interaction. Being mentored is a great way to discuss major life decisions with someone who might have been in a similar position, or is in a position you hope to be in the future. Mentors show you how to lead. And when you've made it yourself, becoming a mentor is a great way to pay it forward and help mold a young individuals future for the better.

Role Model

Having role models can be incredibly useful in modeling your decisions and behavior after. It is often someone who you'd switch lives with in a heartbeat, but since that's unlikely, you'll settle for admiring from a distance. And the difference between a mentor and a role model is usually distance. You most likely do not know them on a personal level, but rather someone you admire, and hope to mirror your decisions on. If someone were to ask me whom I see as my role model(s), I'd have to say Hillary Clinton and Beyoncé Knowles. Both strong independent woman who know what they want and aren't afraid to go after it. However, the likelihood of them becoming my personal friend is slim, *but a girl can always hope.*

And the final category in the personal development field is volunteering, one of the most admirable goals on a bucket list.

Volunteer / Community Service
I'm so happy to see many volunteer and community based goals on so many bucket lists. It's funny how when you channel your time and energy toward others, you gain so much more. Volunteering is a fantastic way to give back to your community, locally and even internationally. Have you ever wanted to volunteer at an elephant rescue charity? Or help build houses with Habitat for Humanity? Volunteer-Tourism was meant for bucket lists. You'll feel great about helping the world, get to meet some amazing people, and experience cultures that are pretty unique.

If you're thinking of volunteering abroad, check out Laura's experience. If this isn't inspiring, I don't know what is.

Volunteering Abroad

I traveled to India with a family-sized group of young people, all around my age. We ventured into the cities and trekked through the countryside traversing the many varied areas of India. It was the most life altering experiences I have ever had because India is such an intense and full place. The way people live in that country is unique to anywhere I have been. It is such a comprehensive sample of what human life really is: the suffering, the joy, the filth and the beauty all rolled into one single offering.

In a twist of fate, we were scheduled to volunteer at one of the most highly regarded facilities in India and the world: The Mother Theresa Home for the Destitute in Kolkata (or Calcutta). Although our group had bonded over the weeks of our initial travels, we were independently partaking in our journey. So, when choosing what particular area to work in at that center, I just went with my feelings. I was inclined to work with mentally diseased women. It was an intriguing area of human life for me: the challenge of their state, mixed with the comfort of womanhood led me down that path. Maybe I also was interested because I knew that my own grandmother had been schizophrenic for much of her life, yet I never experienced it firsthand.

Interestingly enough, I was the only foreigner from around sixty who chose that destination. It only made my experience richer. I was bombarded. As I pushed through the large and aged door of the building into the open courtyard, women of all ages and sizes, yet all wearing loose medical gowns, began to slowly enclose around me. I was smiling, trying to be strong over my nervousness, and introduce myself to the ladies. They touched me and some put their faces too close to mine. There was no one in charge that I found for the first hour of my time there. I wandered and investigated the medical facility, I peeked into large sleeping quarters, and I sat with women and held their hands.

At last I was welcomed by a nun, but instead of sharing in the overwhelming feelings of being amongst the mentally challenged crowd, she seemed numb to their antics, and hurried in directing my duties.

My breath came at one break a day, when I stayed outside the women's building and snacked on chai and English biscuits with a couple volunteers from the surrounding buildings. Although the nourishment was excellent and abundant, I couldn't wait to go back into the jungle of women at my station.

That experience made me feel whole. India had showed me its intricate and complete face through my travels thus far, but at that volunteer site I began to feel my own skin. I was the only foreigner joining the world that the women and nuns called their life. I was able to talk amongst them, and see firsthand how things worked, without anyone speaking to me in a familiar American accent or giving me Westernized glances of distaste or amazement. It was just me in this hot and deeply Indian environment, day in and day out. It was the best time of my life in many ways. Some women danced and jumped with me for too long, but it was acceptable and the fun never ended.

One quiet girl showed me her "homework" with pride and I felt honored that she chose to put her confidence in me like that. There was a think gray-haired woman who sat on the floor or lay in her bed and never uttered a sound other than the putter of her labored breath. She seemed to be almost one hundred, and I sat with her, admiring her weathered skin, the lines and creases speaking like rings of a tree trunk, yet with emotion, despair, and richness.

I became comfortable in their excitement, their strange looks, and their words that came from a million directions. I felt at ease and enjoyed their commotion. They became like friends during those days of volunteering. I realized how many levels of human understanding really exist, or at least I discovered more than I had known. I learned how flexible humans can be, and how able we are to endure and adapt to situations. I had found the craziness and simultaneous acceptance of India in me[15].

What you can do to make these goals stick

This chapter did start off on a little bit of a sour note. Most resolutions don't stick. They are simply too vague to succeed. As humans, we get discouraged and jaded over time, eventually just giving up. But there's hope. Just think of the experiences to come if you stick to your goals. Here are a few of our favorite things to do to make your bucket list goals stick:

Why Resolutions Fail

---

[15] http://bucketlist.org/discover/volunteer-abroad/

Resolutions have evolved into a phenomenon with over half of the population setting goals for the year to come. Most notably:

- weight loss
- quitting smoking/drinking
- budgeting
- financial goals
- career advancement
- relationship goals

But staggeringly, just 8% of people keep their resolutions. Resolutions get a bad rap because they are set with the wrong state of mind. But once a difficult patch hits, it's easier to give up than picking yourself up to continue. The underlining reason we see so many goals fail is because there is a lack of effort in the planning stage of goal setting.

Picking the ultimate goal you want to hit is great and an important part of the goal setting process, but it is a process. Think of it as step 1.

Choose one goal
Bucket lists should be long and continually growing, but sometimes all that 'crazy-awesomeness' may become a little overwhelming. My advice? Choose one goal at a time. Something that excites you, but something you can easily break down into a SMART goal.

Step by step, day by day
Take your goal and break it down into mini goals or targets. Personally, I am training to run a 10km race by the end of April (I don't like running). But one of the things that keeps me going is the training schedule, broken down into three runs a week. It has really helped me focus on the little

milestones along the way. At first running a 10km seemed nearly impossible for someone like me, but after completing about a month of training, my goal seemed within reach.

Hold Yourself Accountable – tell a friend
Some goals are private, and are for you alone, but for the ones you are ready to share, tell a friend, and have him or her tell you theirs. It truly is amazing how much the power of sharing your goals has.

Keep on, Keepin' on
Finally, remember to keep moving forward. If you mess up a week, don't beat yourself up; after all, you're only human. The best way to get over the failures is to celebrate the victories. You run a mile without stopping? Celebrate! Booked your flights? Celebrate! Wrote down your bucket list goals? Celebrate! After all, life is all about the little things. Personal goals have endless possibilities.

Here are our 10 favorite goals.

Top 10 Personal Development Bucket List Goals

1. Run a Marathon

2. Learn a New Language

3. Do a Color Run

4. Volunteer Abroad

5. Get a Driver's License

6. Learn to Play the Piano

7. Graduate University

8. Make a Difference in the World

9. Get a Promotion

10. Learn How to Fly a Helicopter

FAMILY & RELATIONSHIPS

"The love of family and the admiration of friends is much more important than wealth and privilege."
- *Charles Kuralt*

Love. Love is a beautiful and powerful emotion. So powerful, it is often the focus and inspiration of quite a few bucket list items. Whether to fall in love, do something remarkable for your loved one or complete a bucket list together, relationships are the cornerstone of a good family bucket list and the building blocks of many memories to come.

In case you missed it earlier, one of my favorite stats on successful goal setting practices says:

> People who write down their goals, and share them with friends to be more accountable are over 33% MORE successful than people that just write them down.[16]

Accomplishing bucket list items is a great bonding experience. There is nothing quite like defying danger to

---

[16] http://www.dominican.edu/dominicannews/study-backs-up-strategies-for-achieving-goals

really grow closer to a friend or loved one. I find it funny that bucket lists have this stigma as deeply egotistic, private, intimate and *even* selfish! But that couldn't be further from the truth. On 99% of the bucket lists we see, there are at least a couple goals that are directed at either helping someone out, or spoiling a loved one. For example, nearly 3,000[17] people want to take their mother on a vacation of her dreams.

Why completing your bucket list with someone makes you more successful

An Indiana University study showed that after one year, the dropout rate for a fitness program was only 8% for those who had joined with a partner, compared to roughly 50% among people who joined the program alone[18]. It all boils down to accountability. When you fail, and hopefully it doesn't happen too often, who are you letting down? Yourself. But if you commit to a goal with a friend or family member, liability and obligation are added to your goal. Overall, friendship and the bond you feel achieving a goal together is infinitely better than just doing it alone. Finally, there is one more super important reason for having a bucket list buddy: it's a lot of fun. Like way more fun than being alone. Want to learn the guitar? Take the class with your best friend, prepare yourselves for celebrity, and become guitar heroes.

17

http://bucketlist.org/search/?q=Take%20my%20mom%20o
n%20the%20vacation%20of%20her%20dreams
[18] http://experiencelife.com/article/strength-in-numbers-the-importance-of-fitness-buddies/

By taking on the mentality that there is "strength in numbers," it allows you to create a fantastic support system. When you're feeling defeated or stuck in a rut, your support system can give you advice, or even just the encouragement that you need to succeed. At the very least, couples who commit to kicking bad habits together are more successful. In fact, "50% of women successfully quit smoking if their partner stopped at the same time!"[19]

Types of popular relationship categories

Whether you have goals with your loved ones or for your loved ones, we see a few popular sub-categories that emerge.

Romance
Let's start with a gushy goal, romance. Nearly 7,000 people just want to fall in love – hey, maybe we should start a bucket list dating service. And from most of our research, we see that people don't want any of that puppy love nonsense; they want the head over heels, *The Notebook* level love. The kind of love that makes the cynical even sicker.

Family
"A phenomenal life changing experience. We became complete on the day our sweet son was born. He was and is our miracle child and we will forever be grateful for the opportunity to be his mommy and daddy. Adoption is a journey if love, it can be overwhelming but beyond worth it."

Brooke's moving quote gives us a glimpse of the joys of adopting children, a gift that runs deeper than anything I could ever say. Starting a family will change your life. It

---

[19] http://www.torontosun.com/2015/01/20/couples-who-kick-bad-habits-together-more-successful-study

doesn't have to just be a child either; as a new pet parent, I finally understand the responsibility you feel to another life. Taking the family bond to the next level through a bucket list is a great way to not only teach and align what you value in life, but also have amazing once-in-a-lifetime experiences with the people you love. Don't ever think your parents or grandparents are too old or boring to do something crazy with you. Chances are, back in "their day" they were just as bright eyed and wild.

As we mentioned earlier, one of the most popular bucket list goals is to take your mom and dad on the vacation of their dreams. Most children want to give back to their parents and thank them for all of the hard work and patience they've given them. Take a read at Darren's heartwarming story when he and his mom embarked on the vacation of her dreams.

"My mum has had a pretty rough couple of years. At only 56 she has developed early stages of Osteoarthritis, which she deals with using a pain management course of different painkillers to stop it getting too bad. To top that off, she was involved in a car accident in August 2013, adding whiplash to that mix. The following month, she started getting blurred and blocked vision, and she discovered she has torn retinas, which will inevitably detach, at which point she will need a speedy operation to avoid losing her sight. With all this bad stuff going on I knew it was the right time to give her something to look forward to. Mum had just a couple of things I was aware of on her own bucket list, one of which was to visit Rome, so I decided to book us a break away to give her something good to look forward to. I'm pleased to say she had an amazing time and was a very happy mummy. It was great to be able to treat her and see her having a lovely time."[20]

Friendship

Finally, it's often said friends are the family we choose. So many bucket list goals include achieving a goal with a best friend. It is simply a great way to keep yourself happy and on track. When you feel accountability toward someone you're especially close with, letting him or her down is probably not even an option. Plus crushing your bucket list with your best friend can be some of the most fun and rewarding goals you ever achieve.

Use your relationships to make separate bucket list goals with the people you love or challenge each other to achieve beautiful and fulfilling things. From the places you want to take your family, to a best friends' ultimate summer bucket list, the possibilities are endless.

Whatever your relationship bucket list goals are, remember they are a fantastic way to build bonds and support each other toward bucket list success. Here are 10 of our favorite

[20] http://bucketlist.org/discover/take-my-mom-on-the-vacation-of-her-dreams/#.VMCMyNx331o

family and relationship bucket list goals for you to achieve and grow the love.

Top 10 Relationship Goals

1. Fall in love

2. Take my parents on their dream vacation

3. Road trip with friends

4. Take a photo of myself everyday for a year

5. Have a baby

6. Have a family reunion

7. Throw a surprise party

8. Bungee Jump with Grandparents

9. Start a Memory Jar

10. Be a Maid of Honor

UNIQUE GOALS

"Don't compare yourself with anyone in this world...if you do so, you are insulting yourself."
- Bill Gates

Finally, we find that there are goals too special to fall under a singular category. Like we said before, a bucket list is personal and unique to the individual – as it should be. This is your opportunity to create some beautiful, funny and meaningful goals that are distinct to you!

By now you've probably realized that I am not the most extreme person out there, so some of my own bucket list goals are a bit "unique" to me. But hear me out! Some things that seem boring to one person can be a life changing activity to another. Just take a recent trip to the Calgary Stampede this summer, where a trip to a bar turned into a bucket list goal in the making.

Singing Karaoke Alone
Have you ever listened to Beyoncé and thought, "Yes, I think it's time for me to become a world-class, famous singer." Well, nine days out of 10 I do. But if I can let you into a little secret, my voice is about as smooth and seductive as a dying cat. So what is a person – *with the soul of Aretha but the voice of Kermit the frog* - supposed to do? Karaoke, of course! It wasn't until a recent trip to Calgary that I realized how daunting

singing solo can be – so I thought for all you wallflowers, here is a little bucket list story about my karaoke experience and why singing solo on the karaoke stage has to be on your bucket list too.

It all started on a Friday evening, as too many stories do. We were excited to be in Calgary, Alberta, Canada for the Stampede and were ready to soak up the electricity the Stampede brings to Calgary. Turns out a *lot* of other people had the same idea and a lot of classic establishments were packed to the brim. Being a group of 14 (yes, somehow we managed to round up 14 friends for the trip), we were a little difficult to accommodate – to say the least. Luckily, we had a couple of local Calgarians with us, and the inclination to make fools of ourselves.

We found a little gem, Ducky's Bar, almost as if it were drawing us in. With a slightly rough exterior, but all the charm of an original karaoke establishment, we sat down. This wasn't any old karaoke dive bar, though. This was going to be the place where I accomplished a dream and crossed off a bucket list goal. To be completely honest with you, I have sung karaoke before, but never by myself.

Flipping through the giant book of songs, I spotted something that I knew would lead to my karaoke destiny. Surprisingly, it wasn't Beyoncé, it was Garth Brooks, "Friends in Low Places." I love my friends, I really do, but this is the song of our friendship (in a good way). I wrote down my name, the song name and handed it to the karaoke master. Waiting for my name to be called felt like an eternity, and what made it oh-so-much-worse was the fact that nearly every other 'singer' seemed to be straight off of a professional tour.

Finally after a few glasses of liquid courage and Adele's "Skyfall" (she actually sounded like Adele...) my name was announced! Standing on stage and staring out into an audience of friends and strangers is a scary feeling, but I was excited. When the first three chords were struck, my table of hooligans erupted as they figured out which song I was going to sing – our song.

Needless to say I wasn't entirely singing alone, as the whole bar erupted at the chorus. It will be one of those memories I will always remember. I've realized that it doesn't really matter how you sound; if you're confident and have great friends singing backup, karaoke by yourself will become one of those great life stories that will last you the rest of your life.

What I love most about these special and unique types of goals is that they tend to be some of the most memorable accomplishments on your bucket list. They're usually sporadic, mischievous and a lot of fun to do.

Check out some of our favorite 'special' bucket list goals:

Top 10 Special Bucket List Goals

DO EPIC SH*T

1. Shave a Coconut

2. Cover a Car in Post-it Notes

3. Laugh Until You Cry

4. Buy the Person Behind You a Coffee

5. Draw Funny Faces on Every Egg in the Carton

6. Have the Ultimate Water Fight

7. Dye Your Hair a Crazy Color

8. Write a Letter to Yourself and Open it in 10 Years

9. Dance in the Rain

10. Own a Polydactyl Cat

PART 3 – Let's Travel the World

"All travel has its advantages. If the passenger visits better countries, he may learn to improve his own. And if fortune carries him to worse, he may learn to enjoy it."

– Samuel Johnson

BUCKETLIST'S GUIDE TO TRAVELING THE WORLD

"One's destination is never a place, but a new way of seeing things."
– Henry Miller

I can't tell you the last time I saw a plane and didn't wish I were on it, travelling to a fantastic location, ready to embark on a new adventure of a lifetime. Sadly, right now, I can only dream. But for you, if you're ready to be the person staring out the window at the world, which looks oh-so-simple from up there, it's time to take your life to the next level. Earlier, we looked at why travel is so awesome – like you needed any more convincing – but now it's time to share with you some of the best tips collected from all over the world, to kick start your bucket list travels and adventures. From saving money, to packing like a pro, by the time you're finished with this part of the book, you'll be booking your ticket around the world – and not going bankrupt because of it.

Before the trip – taking the leap

Taking on an adventure alone is a scary thing. The first time I decided to travel on my own I was shaking in my boots - really. No longer are your parents there to hold your hands, or friends there to lean on for support. And if I'm completely honest, I'm not the most outgoing person when I first meet new people; in fact, at first I think I come off a little standoffish and shy. But I assure you the fact is you won't be alone for long, *you will make friends* and you will make them in no time. It's time to shake away the fear and put yourself out there. There really is no time like the present to start your life's adventure. Really, what's the point of waiting around for someone else to be ready? It's time to grab the bull by the horns and get doing what you want to do.

Whether you travel for two weeks, two months, two years, or just to start checking off that mile long bucket list, use some of the information to come to help plan and budget for your adventure. After all, the biggest regrets come from the chances we didn't take, not the ones we did.

SAVING YOUR MONEY

"Tourists don't know where they've been, travelers don't know where they're going."
– Paul Theroux

Here's the truth, travelling is going to cost you money, but the good thing is, it's not as scary – or expensive – as you think if you're smart about your savings and your spending before, during and after the trip. It's all about priorities and if you're *really* ready to commit to travel. In this section, discover how world travelers fund their adventures *before* the adventure.

Depending on the length of time and where you go determines how much you should have put away for your travels. We compiled a handy chart on the next page with the 30 most popular bucket list worthy destinations and their average cost per night. Of course, this is just an estimate, but it is a great place to start your budget. I recommend using the chart as a starting point to your expenses for the trip.

The list below is selected from Travel Eye. They conducted a survey with participants from all over the world and extracted the top travel destinations. [21]

In coming up with the cost per day, we took into consideration, food, transportation, lodging, activities and, of course, a little extra for spending on adventure tourism activities. All costs are in U.S. dollars to help make your estimates easier. The costs below may also seem like a jump from the typical backpackers guide, but we factored in activities and attractions as well, an additional cost that is sometimes overlooked in the traditional backpackers travel guides.

Sydney, Australia	$100
London, England	$250
Paris, France	$175
Venice, Italy	$125
New York, NY, USA	$200
Cape Town, SA	$140
Las Vegas, USA	$200
Rome, Italy	$160
South Island, New Zealand Region	$110
San Francisco, USA	$175
Rio De Janeiro, Brazil	$110
Dubai, UAE	$300
Auckland, New Zealand	$100
Singapore, Asia	$120
Phuket Thailand	$90
Bali, Indonesia	$65

2121http://www.traveleye.com/client/top100.php#sthash.7aM 0Ifpw.dpuf

Durban, South Africa	$50
Bangkok, Thailand	$50
Vancouver, Canada	$80
Cairns, Australia	$100
Melbourne, Australia	$100
Cairo, Egypt	$50
Madrid, Spain	$145
Dodoma, Tanzania	$90
Suva, Fiji	$100
Amsterdam, Netherlands	$160
Agra, India	$40
Beijing, China	$75
Berlin, Germany	$130
Glasgow, Scotland	$175

As you can see, European countries will most likely cost you close to or over $100 a day, on average, whereas Southeast Asia can be as low as $40.

If you're planning on traveling around the world, it's important to be prepared for price differences in cities and have the appropriate budget in each. On the other hand, we know that in cities like Phuket and Agra you shouldn't be spending more than a mere $50 a day. In fact, in these cities, that is even a high estimate.

I'm going to sound like your mama here, but remember to always be smart. Traveling is an amazing thing, but sometimes people do not always have your best interests at heart, and if they see you as a scam-able/gullible tourist, chances are they will either try to oversell or flat out take advantage of you. Travel smart and be prepared to know what things should cost you.

Tips for saving for your travels

I once read a quote – and if you're a fan of Pinterest or Tumblr I'm sure you've seen it too – that said,

"Travel is the only thing you buy that makes you richer." - Anonymous

A bit of a soppy sentiment, but you get the point. Travelling is an investment in your well being as a human. But with any investment, sacrifice is sometimes essential. Here are a few of our favorite money saving actions you can take to start pinching the pennies now, to live an amazing bucket list life later.

First thing I would recommend is to use a personal finance tracker. Apps such as Mint make budgeting a cinch, and it is free to download. Finding out where your finances stand to start with will make it easier to see where you can cut back and save. I'm suggesting Mint because it is the app that I personally use. It is easy – and safe – to connect your banking information to, and it creates handy charts to see where you spend your money. It can sometimes be a bit of an eye-opener, especially when I saw the money I was spending on coffee each week. It's a fantastic place to start because you can track your spending and evaluate where your expenses are heading.

Once you begin to see where your finances lie, it becomes a little easier to see where you can start saving money. For me, just saving the money I would spend on coffee or buying lunch was a great place to cut back. Additionally, rent, coffee, eating out, and sadly booze are some great places to cut back and put away. If you are truly committed to having an ultimate journey, giving up some freedoms like living on your own is a key place to save the money you'll need to travel.

Moving in with your family or staying with a good, *good* friend for a few months before your journey can save you upwards of $1800 - $2000 depending on where you live – a low estimate if you're in Vancouver like I am. Travelling in Southeast Asia, $2000 is equivalent to almost 40–50 days of worry-free enjoyment! Eating out and drinking are also budget busters. Choose a number that you want to save up and stick to it. The rewards are far greater than a regular old night out with your coworkers and friends. Remember the goal setting habits I discussed in the early chapters of this book? Evaluating why you want to travel and reaffirming it to yourself on a regular basis will help with keeping you on track to the jet-setting lifestyle of your dreams.

Finally, if you are a working professional, chances are you probably have some unique and talented skills. Try contracting yourself out to take on a few additional hours of work a week. On sites such as O-desk you can pick up contracted work where the earnings from each project could go directly to your travel fund. With the additional income you'll have the funds you need in no time – potentially without even changing your current lifestyle.

Even if you start to put $50 away from every paycheck, you'll have saved $1200 in only a year. From my experience, once you begin cutting back and experiencing how other cultures live, you'll realize how much excess surrounds us all, and you'll begin to question your spending habits on the regular.

DO EPIC SH*T

MANAGING YOUR MONEY WHILE YOU'RE AWAY

"A journey is best measured in friends, rather than miles."
— Tim Cahill

Managing your money while traveling can be difficult for many reasons. Maybe you're not good at budgeting or you have a hard time dealing with foreign currency. For me, I have a hard time paying for things in cash. Not that I can't, or don't know how, but when I'm at home 99% of the time I use a card and it's rare that carry around bills or coins to buy things with. While most places, especially in Europe, and other big cities around the world, are likely to accept cards, carrying the local currency saves time and money in the long run. Know how much cash to carry in a day and how to get the most from your dollar when you're away.

Getting Foreign Currency

Convert your money before you go
If you're heading to one country, converting your currency before you go is a smart and often cost-saving approach to travelling. Your bank can often provide the best exchange rates with minimal fees on your conversion. And if you've set your estimated budget before you go, you can exchange the amount you expect to spend all in one go.

Stop at the local ATM

If your plans include many different countries – which means many different currencies – then there's no better, cheaper, easier way to get a specific currency than in that country. You'll get the best exchange rate, and if you have a good debit card, you won't get charged at the ATM either, and you really aren't paying just to get money. But be wary of your banks' fees when withdrawing money overseas. Sometimes there can be a lot of hidden fees. If this is your primary method of converting currency, I recommend withdrawing large quantities of money at a time to avoid the fees.

Traveler's Checks

I know I probably don't even have to say this, but they are a definite no. A lot of people still think traveler's checks are a thing. But if I'm being honest, I've never seen a traveler's check since my parents used them in the early 90's. I wouldn't know what it was if I found a stack of them on the streets.

Exchange Offices

If you have cash you need to change, it's not impossible. There are plenty of places in most big cities, and even banks. Just do your research first. Check online to see what the most current exchange rate is and make sure wherever you go is legitimate and doesn't charge you, because sometimes the hidden fees can make converting your currency abroad a nightmare.

Setting a budget on the trip

Write out all expected expenses

The way to start any budget is to figure out what you are going to buy and spend on a daily basis as best as you can. Write what you have already paid for, then what you've reserved, like hotels, tours, car rental, and what you know you're going to pay for - train tickets, public transport etc.

And finally give yourself an allowance per day, or if you have more leeway with your budget, per week. The benefits of having a budget are extreme: you won't be surprised by how much you're spending, you'll be more conscious of your purchases, you can travel for longer and you can make better choices.

Keep track of your daily spending

Again, depending on how strict your budget is, try to keep track on a regular basis of how much you're spending when you're on your travels. Especially if traveling with someone, you can tend to pay for each other and say, "It'll even out." No doubt it will, somehow, but keeping track assures that you are paying your share and being smart with your money.

Keeping Your Money Safe

Whether it's your first or tenth time travelling, keeping your money and other valuables safe needs to be a priority. Like I said before, sometimes people don't have your best interest at heart when they see you as a vulnerable tourist. I learned this the hard way on a subway in Barcelona. I got on the train with a full wallet and a happy heart, but when I got off I was one wallet short in my handbag. Let's just say I learned my lesson fast. Here are some easy tips to follow to keep your money safe while abroad.

Don't carry a large amount of cash

This is pretty standard wherever you are. You don't want to carry too much in case something goes wrong. If you are mugged, pick pocketed, or you lose it, it won't be too much. And always have an emergency fund in a different location.

Don't count your money in public
Again, this is something that you probably know, but it's good to remember. Counting your money, or just having it out in the open is like an invitation. Just discretely count it right in front of the ATM when you take it out, but put it right away. Walking down the street while counting and trying to put it away is not a great idea.

Don't carry all of your money on you
This is the same as not carrying a large amount of cash with you. Leave some cash or even an emergency credit card with your other belongings in a safe or a secret place. Luckily when I was in Barcelona, I had an emergency fund in my bag at the hotel, so I could continue on with my travels.

Other Tips

Write down important numbers
In case you lose your credit card, write down the number to call so you're not scrambling to figure it out while also worrying about the lost wallet.

Make a copy of your credit card
This will make sure you have the correct card number and information. Having the picture too, not just the numbers written down can be another way to show it's actually your card. Keep copies in different places, and one at home, just in case.

Banking and Currency Abroad

Now, are you a first time traveler? There are some strategies and tips you can take to protect your hard earned money and savings while you're away.

Let me start by telling you a little story about credit cards. When I was in my senior year of high school, we took a grad trip to Spain and France with about thirty students and five chaperones. This trip was an annual rite of passage for a lot of the graduating class, and had been taken every year for a while. And before I get too far with the story, this was also a lot of the students' first time leaving the country. With all the meetings and preparation, you'd think one key discussion would revolve around credit cards - *it didn't*.

On one of the first days, feeling like little independent adults, we were allowed to go off on our own for the afternoon. Paris at any age is simply magical, but with its classic old world charm comes the winding streets, which is confusing to navigate at any age. Especially for a group of 18 year olds who are used to a city with three major streets in its downtown.

Anyway, this was quite a few years back and Citibikes were just beginning to pop up in major European cities and for 1€ you could cruise around the city of love. The bikes operated by inserting your credit card, which unlocks a bike, and if you return the bike you only get charged the 1€.

Well, one of my good friends was the only one of us who had a credit card, and since four bucks isn't such a big expense, she agreed to put them on her card so we could ride around Paris like the tourists of our dreams. Turns out she forgot one fatal detail before she left, which was to let her bank know she was travelling abroad. Now this was the time before smart phones could connect to wifi at the drop of a hat, and it was fairly difficult to contact home unless you were at the hotel. But you guessed it, her bank thought her card was stolen, automatically froze it, so she couldn't put any more expenses on it, and she was stuck in a foreign country with about 100 Euros to her name.

Long story short, the first rule of traveling is to let your bank know you're travelling. Simple enough, but it can affect your entire trip if you're no longer able to access your credit card.

And while we're on the topic of credit cards, travel reward cards have a lot of benefits to an adventurer. I'm not an expert by any means, but using points to purchase things like your flights just makes sense. Most travel rewards credit cards work by providing you with a certain amount of reward points for every dollar spent. Of course the credit card company is always going to win, so you have to be responsible as ever with credit to avoid overspending, but if you begin to charge your everyday purchases and expenses to your card, the points will add up.

Cards versus Cash

There is always a debate about the best form of currency to carry when travelling. In my opinion, a mixture of credit/debit cards and cash is the safest way to travel to prevent paying extortionate fees and duties. Avoid converting your money at airports or highly touristy areas, and hit up only reputable ATMs once you're at your destination.

FLIGHTS AND TRANSPORTATION

"Like all great travelers, I have seen more than I remember, and remember more than I have seen."
— *Benjamin Disraeli*

Flying is expensive; it's probably going to be one of your biggest expenses of the trip. Booking the flight is also probably one of the biggest hurdles you need to overcome when taking the first step in your travels. From experience, I've learned that there are a couple of key ways of getting around without breaking the bank.

For your flights, there are two main ways to get to your destination. First, you can book a single ticket to a city, travel around that area and book a return flight back to your home. Alternatively, you can take the ultimate step to an astounding adventure, an around the world ticket. With an around the world ticket, you have the opportunity to visit a lot of countries at a more affordable option because you usually stick with one airline company or conglomerate. Both have benefits depending on what you want out of your adventure, where you're traveling, and how long you plan on being away. However be aware that an around the world ticket can run from $2,700 to $10,000 depending on your destinations.

Conventional Airfare

If you're not quite ready to commit to an around the world ticket, there are some things you should know about purchasing conventional airfare, whether it's to another city or another continent.

Buy early or buy late
If you're ready to truly take on an adventure, of course buy your ticket early. Flights typically go up two weeks before travelling, especially during peak season. You can save a lot of money by booking your flights three to six months in advance. Conversely, if you have luck on your side, and have a spontaneous gene, booking late can also save you money. If airlines have failed to fill to capacity, airlines will sell tickets at some incredible prices instead of seeing those seats go to waste. Many major airlines and travel websites have "Last Minute Deals" prominently displayed on their homepage. If you have the ability to leave at the drop of a hat, do it.

Shop around
Buying your plane ticket is a big chunk of change, although the first site you look at may seem like an incredible deal, it's always a good idea to check all the major competitors. Use Google's Flights search feature (google.com/flights) to easily compare different airlines. In fact, they create a handy graph showing which dates are cheapest to fly on. A pro tip is to search for deals with your private on incognito browsing on. This blocks websites from viewing or tracking your browsing history. It's rumored that travel sites increase pricing based on how many times you've viewed a flight or vacation. Even if it's not 100% fact, it's an easy prevention to take.

Know when to buy, know when to fly
Traditionally, flight sales will start on a Tuesday. Coincidentally, Tuesday and Wednesdays are also the

cheapest days to fly because they are the least busy days of the week.

Sites to use to research your Travels

I don't have to tell you that times have changed, and the Internet is the primary place to research and plan your travels. The travel industry has exploded online in recent years, and with it there are quite a few fantastic resources to research and book online. Here are a few of our favorite sites:

Flights

Skyscanner
This is probably one of my favorite websites to search for flights. I might not always book through them, instead booking the airline's site, but I always check here first because I've found the flights to be cheap and a really good baseline.

Cheapoair
Cheapoair.com is another great alternative to find flights at a cheap price. It searches over 450 airlines to find the best flights.

Kayak
It's a great place to view multiple deals in one spot.

Try setting fare price alerts with sites like airfarewatchdog.com to track if a flight you're interested in drops. And recently a new service called Flightfox charges a flat rate of $49 where a panel of travellers find you the best deal there is, guaranteed. I haven't used the service myself, but it seems like a great service for anyone booking large adventures.

On The Ground Transportation

Getting around when you're in a foreign country can be difficult at best; a tip we always find useful and frugal is to do as the locals would do. In other words, your best bet for saving funds is to take transit. Alternatively, check out the resources below to help plan your on the ground transportation.

Uber
You've probably heard a lot about Uber recently, and for good reason. It's an easy and affordable service. And it's synced with your credit card, so no need to feel obligated to tip, or carry extra cash around.

Bus Travel

Student Agency
They go all over Europe and they're a great value.

Greyhound
Traveling around Canada or the U.S.? Nothing beats a Greyhound for cost efficiency. Although it's not the most comfortable mode of transportation, it is cheap and air-conditioned.

Accommodation

If you're a true traveler, hostels are the best place to stay at the most effective price. Not only do you get your accommodation, but also they often put on events like pub-crawls, and tours for their guests, a great place to meet new people.

Booking.com
Especially for hostels use them to know what you're getting into. The reviews provide great insight into your accommodation that you otherwise wouldn't know. And you can have a profile that saves your bookings right in one place.

Airbnb
This is a great site for renting homes for short periods, or long if it's available. I've stayed in a few homes through Airbnb and I have had really great experiences. You can see ratings and how many times they've rented their home before to make sure you are staying in a clean and safe environment. You can also use Airbnb when you're away to make some extra cash to subsidize your travel, just make sure you're allowed to with your building or landlord.

Hostelbookers
They have great profiles on hostels around the world, which is an easy way to get other tips and reviews on your accommodations before you even leave for the airport.

ADVENTURES TOURISM

"The very basic core of a man's living spirit is his
passion for adventure."
- *Christopher McCandless*

Now that we have some of the traditional aspects of your travels discussed, it's time to turn your vacation into an adventure – let's talk about your bucket list. When you're on the road, there really is no better time to seek out and check off the bucket list goals you've always dreamed of.

P.S. If you're ready to dive into making your own bucket list, have a look at the next part of this book. We've shared with you the top 25 goals from Bucketlist.org and why we think they are pretty special.

Completing your bucket list on the road

While traveling is a gift in and of itself, why not set out to complete some of your other bucket list goals while you are away? So much of your trip can revolve around once-in-a-lifetime opportunities that just aren't available in your town, state, or even country. The key is planning these bucket list trips before you go. You can save a lot of time and money in doing so. And it really boils down to doing some impeccable research and planning.

Tourist Attractions

Tourist attractions are vital to many cities' economies and are woven into their cultural fabric. It's for a reason. Usually steeped in so much history and tradition, it's no wonder it draws in a big crowd. But of course with the pull of these ancient and beautiful artifacts comes the draw to rip off foreigners. By planning out where you're going to go, and how you're going to get there beforehand, you can avoid falling in the dreaded tourist trap. Remember, during peak season, even water prices can be marked up 75-100% of their actual cost with the large volume of people.

Around these incredible landmarks also draws a lot of not so savory vendors. Be wary of the knock off industry. In some countries you can get heavily penalized for purchasing from the street.

Tour Companies

STA Travel
I haven't gone through their tours personally, but I like their ISIC card, which allows you to get discounts from Amtrak tickets to random museums around the world. There are also other cards for teachers and those students as long as you're under 26.

City Discovery - I used this company to book a tour to Blarney Castle in Ireland. I thought it was a good tour. There are tons of tours, either day tours or longer ones, all over the world.

95

Contiki

Of course for young-adults Contiki is one of the best tours around. However, it does run on the more expensive side. On one hand, you don't need to worry about anything, because everything is practically included in the trip. On the other hand, it can be a little constricting for the free spirits in all of us.

Bucketlist

Finally, I'd be remiss if I didn't mention bucketlist.org. It's a fantastic database of ideas for all areas of the world. With over 3 million ideas, you can search for your destination and discover what the locals do. And you can read reviews of how people accomplished their adventures, tips on what to do, and ratings on what is and isn't worth seeing.

GENERAL TIPS AND RESOURCES FOR TRAVELERS

"Travel is glamorous only in retrospect."
— *Paul Theroux*

Booking a trip to an exotic location is an exciting time in any young traveler's life ... until it's time to pack. Over-pack and you're stuck lugging a heavy backpack or (worse) a suitcase around for hours at a time. Under-pack and you're left having to shell out some of your hard earned cash in order to survive.

Before you go, remember these tips:

- Research the culture
- Check the weather
- Make a list – check it twice
- Don't wait until the last minute
- Think in outfits instead of individual items
- Lay everything out before putting it in your bag or suitcase
- Put away at least 1/4 of what you have out. You won't need it

. Don't leave too much room for "extras," you'll end up packing or bringing back more than you actually need

10 Words or Phrases to Remember

If you're traveling to a non-English speaking part of the world, it is important to make an effort to learn cultural practices and local language. I find the language barrier the toughest part about traveling to another country. You can learn to eat different foods, you can use different bathrooms, and you can live differently than at home. But not knowing a language will keep you at a distance from those around you unless you can find some common language or another way to communicate. And while it's impossible to learn every language, no matter how much time you have, you can at least learn the basics so you show the people you're *at least* attempting to learn their language, and hopefully not get in any small misunderstandings that are cleared up by knowing a few words.

Words to learn before you leave

Hello/Goodbye - I put these together because they're really a pair, and if you're lucky the same word can be used for both.

Good - Saying how you are, how your food is, how your room is, anything. You can avoid using hand gestures where they might be mistaken as vulgar.

Yes/no - These are the easiest words to learn and there's really no excuse not to know them. The locals will most likely thank you for just trying.

Please- Be polite. Depending on where you are they might not know "please" and so won't recognize that you're being polite. Besides, just take it one step further and be more polite by speaking in their language.

Thank you- Same reason as please; manners translate in every language.

5 phrases to learn

How are you? - You'll probably be asked this more than you'll ask it, but it's good to know, that way you don't get hung up right away on the greeting.

I would like - This is the polite way to ask for something, so you're not just pointing like a caveman.

How much is - Again, this is better than a weird hand gesture and shrugging shoulders.

Where is - Maybe you won't understand their answer back, but at least they can point you in the right direction.

Excuse me - This is simply being polite, too.

Why Learn Any of the Language?

Learning some words to use while you're away is a great way to demonstrate that you are trying to adopt their culture. Learning some phrases gives people a good impression of you and prevents you from looking like you're just walking all over them in an ignorant way. With any small group of words you're never going to speak fluently, but you can at least show that you're trying. It's also a badge of honor that you're able to adapt to cultures and countries different than your own.

99

How to get through long flights

You've booked your flights, packed your bags, and are itching to jump into the adventure of a lifetime, but first you have to sit through a 12 hour flight across the world. Some people seem to be naturally great flyers, but the truth is they probably are just frequent flyers. There are a few things to consider when embarking on a long flight. Luckily for you, we have them covered below.

What to wear

Comfy jeans or sweat pants
I usually wear jeans because they can stand up to pretty much anything, but recently I've been known to travel in a good pair of leggings. If you spill something, you can easily get it off or hide it. If they get wrinkly it's not really a big deal, and if you have a good pair, they can be pretty comfortable. Sweat pants are also warm and comfortable for a long journey.

Layer a T-shirt or tank top and sweater
This way when you're warm going through the airport and security you can strip down and be comfortable. But like all airplane, once you take off, temperatures usually drop. Having the option of removing a layer is always better than wishing you had another sweater to wear.

Comfortable, loose-fitting shoes
Even in the summer I always wear socks and shoes while traveling on planes because, of the cold. When travelling long distances, feet and ankles tend to swell up. Having loose fitting shoes will make sure you are not in pain while flying.

Scarf

They are like little blankets around your neck. Or if you're warm they can be scrunched up into a pillow.

What to take on the plane with you

Gum

Weird things to start off, with I know, but gum can be a lifesaver. When flying my ears nearly always pop in the air. Chewing can help prevent that. And if you're stuck in your seat, gum can also freshen your breath – your neighbors will thank you too.

Headphones

Headphones are a crucial in everyday life, never mind when you're stuck on a plane with a crying baby for 8 hours. They cut the noise, and can provide you with sanctuary. Not to mention, the ones they give out either break in five minutes or cost $5.

Book

Some people will tell you to never bring something as heavy and bulky as a book, but depending on how long I'll be gone, I'll always bring one, even if it's just a guidebook. During those hours when I don't have charge on my phone or want to save the battery, reading is a great way I pass the time, and learn about the city I'm going to.

Wet wipes

Wet wipes solve any problem. I use these for my hands, messes around me, removing make up and anything else. I primarily use these to wipe my face sometime during the flight. Not washing your face during normal times can really mess with your skin even if I don't have make-up on. It makes me feel a little cleaner and fresher.

Face and hand lotion

This is really it for my "skin care routine" when flying. I bring face lotion because I get dry during the flight and unscented is usually kinder to the neighbors. Try a tinted moisturizer like a BB cream, especially you ladies. It is the lightest coverage to make you look alive and fresh, even after those long flights.

Advil/Tylenol/Gravol

Nothing is worse than sitting on a flight with a pounding headache – especially if there is a screaming baby behind you. Also if you're prone to motion sickness, don't forget the gravol. It can settle your stomach and make for an easier flight – and coincidentally more relaxing flight.

How to survive a long flight

I try to change my watch and mindset to the time zone I'm going to land in as soon as I step foot on the plane. That way, hopefully, when I get there I'm not totally blindsided by the time. Because of that, if I should be sleeping at that time, I try to sleep, and if I should be awake, I try to stay awake. It's really not a perfect science, but it seems to sort of work.

I find the best way to get through long flights is to relax and remember that it will be over soon. Sometimes when you have to spend 15 hours cooped up it can be an overwhelming and stressful situation, but always remember that you are lucky to be travelling at all. Having perspective on the bigger picture often helps me realize that a few hours of minor discomfort is worth it for the experiences to come.

Top List of Travel Resources

Researching for this book, I came across a lot of travel-focused websites and resources. Below are some of the best websites you can use to plan for your adventures. They are also condensed in the resources section located at the end of this book.

Hotels & Accommodation

Airbnb
I've said it before and I'll say it again, Airbnb is one of the most cost effective ways to see the world – in a comfortable manner. Put in the city you want to visit and the date you'll be there, and choose from a variety of great accommodation.

CouchSurfing.com - Bum a night's sleep on somebody's couch and save hundreds of dollars on hotel costs. CouchSurfing is a worldwide community of amazing hosts and adventurous travelers seeing the world on the cheap. But be wary, only for the very brave among us.

Groupon.com – Don't forget to check groupon for deals for your accommodation. Even if you just want to splurge for one night, sometimes you can find remarkable deals on beautiful hotels and resorts.

Home Exchange - The most comprehensive site for home listings. You list your house on the site, find another house where you'd like to stay, and contact the member to see if they want to trade homes for a bit. This exchange system lets you live like a local in a comfortable house or apartment instead of a tiny and expensive hotel room. Kind of like the movie *The Holiday* but in real life.

Hostel Bookers – A fantastic resource if you're going to be staying in hostels on your adventure. Easiest way to book hostels all over the world. You can find prices, amenities (including pictures), and customer reviews of each location so you know what you're getting before you land. You can also book directly from the site.

Hotwire - Hotwire is a robust site that not only offers some of the best travel deals available, but includes planning tools and tips for a smooth trip. Hotwire's partners offer unsold inventory at big savings and rest assured that Hotwire only works with partners you know and trust.

Kayak - The only place you need to search for discounted airfare. Kayak searches over 140+ airlines and travel agencies (including Orbitz.com, Travelocity.com, Hotwire.com, and other big airfare search engines) to find the best flight deals all in one place.

Orbitz - With Orbitz Price Assurance, you're guaranteed the lowest rate offered by Orbitz. If another customer books the same flight on Orbitz at a lower price, you'll automatically be issued a refund for the difference, which is pretty fantastic. They also offer real time traveler updates to keep you apprised of your flight status.

Priceline - Priceline puts the power of pricing back in your hands by allowing you to name your own price for hotels and pay no booking fees for flights, cars, or vacation packages. The site also offers reviews by travelers to help you make the best travel decision.

Flight

Flights are probably one of the biggest expenses you'll face when planning your bucket list adventures – around the world. Have a look at a few great websites to keep an eye on when booking your flights.

Cheapoflights – If you're looking to cut costs, this website is a fantastic place to start. It also has great deals on car-rents cruises and hotels.

Flightfox – I haven't used Flightfox myself for traveling, but I have heard great things. It's almost like your personal digital travel agent. The service, which was founded by travelers like you, charges a one time fee of $49 and the experts will find you the best flight at the best cost.

Google Flights – I like using Google flights as an initial resource to get a feel of what flights to a city will cost. Using the bar graph view is also a really easy way to compare which days will be the cheapest to fly on.

SeatGuru – SeatGuru is a database of airplane seat configurations by airline. You can get diagrams with notes on where the good (and bad) seats are on the plane. You can see a layout of where the galley is (get your food faster) and where the bathrooms are (stay far away). If you know what type of plane you'll be flying on (ask the airline ticketing agent), and you get to pick your seat, make sure to check out SeatGuru first so you don't pick the bad seat next to the toilets.

Skyscanner – Skyscanner scans the Internet for the cheapest deals for your flights, hotels and car rentals.

TripAdvisor - The biggest online community of travellers. This is the first (and often last) stop for vacation planners. Not only can you book flights, hotels, car rentals, and get tickets for attractions here, but you also get an amazing breadth of reviews and tips from real travellers. The destination guides on TripAdvisor are often much better (more up-to-date and more detailed) than the expensive guide books in your bookstore.

Destination Guides and Travel Communities

Get the lowdown on your locale with destination guides and reviews for what to see and do, how to get around, where to eat and sleep, and information about local customs and processes. The best kind of research you can do is to listen to reviews. They are truly first hand experiences from people just like you. I know I would be lost without the help of Tripadvisor's many forums.

The Backpacker - This community reviews local bars, restaurants, accommodations, attractions, and tours. All reviews are user-submitted, and many places have multiple reviews. It's a pretty cool website to take advantage of.

Lonely Planet – The giant of all things travel, the Lonely Planet guides have been a staple in all travelers backpacks since it's publications. Lonely Planet is renowned for its first-hand approach, up-to-date maps and commitment to providing the best information for travelers. Their authors are professional writers and journalists who nail down all the practical info about a destination then build on that with insider knowledge, thorough reviews, little-known facts and authoritative recommendations. They are the best for a reason, and you should listen to all the advice they have to give.

Timeout City Guides - Time Out is an international multimedia publisher of cultural experiences for urban adventurers. They provide up-to-date and accurate information to help readers remain at the cutting edge of culture. Around the world, their local teams of critics are connected to the very best that their city has to offer. Listings are generated in-house and reviews are completely independent.

WikiTravel - Like Wikipedia.org for locales. Free, complete, and reliable worldwide travel guide written by actual travelers. Great resource for learning about your destination cities before you start planning a trip.

Budget Traveler Magazines and Blogs

These are just some of the best reads on travel. Get travel tips, recommendations and ideas firsthand from travellers. Go to these when you're looking for some inspiration or just want to live vicariously through a fellow adventurer.

About.com Budget Travel - Mark Kahler, About.com's guide to budget travel, posts weekly deals, has tips on finding the cheapest vacation packages and airfare, and has a fantastic series of step-by-step articles on maximizing your travel budget.

The Art of Nonconformity - In the battle against conventional beliefs, Chris Guillebeau's blog focuses on three areas: life, work, and travel. He writes about travel hacking in general and his journeys to more than 25 countries every year. So far he has visited more than 100 countries, and over the next four years intends to visit every country in the world. He's also an esteemed fellow member of LifeRemix.

Budget Travel - Web magazine by Frommer's (the guide book publisher) focused on budget travel. Writers post stories on destinations, budget itineraries, tips for finding cheap flights or accommodations, and more. You can even post your own travel journal, photos or videos, and read others' travel journals. There's a paper magazine version that you can subscribe to ($20 for 20 issues) if you prefer to read your cheap vacation news in print.

Cool Travel Guide - Perpetual globetrotter and travel writer Lara Dunston has traveled to over 60 countries, authored and updated over 40 guidebooks, and has had scores of articles published by top travel mags and sites. This blog is about the things that are cool about travel, the things that inspire us to travel, and what's inspiring about travel.

Perceptive Travel - Perceptive Travel is an online travel magazine filled with unique perspectives from around the globe, written by some of the best travel writers on the planet. Come here for authentic travel tales about interesting places, not for top-10 lists and tourism bureau advertorials.

The Professional Hobo - Nora Dunn sold her lucrative financial planning business, sold all her stuff, and embarked on a round-the-world vagabonding life. She shares her adventures on this fun site. (Nora is also a Senior Writer for Wise Bread and contributed lots of financial planning and budget travel articles to our money saving book.)

Song of the Open Road - Currently on year nine of his global journey, Wade has ventured through over 30 countries on five continents, sometimes moving slow, sometimes moving fast. It's obvious that travel is his passion.

Travelvice - In December 2005, Craig Heimburger sold most of his possessions and took off for an extended travel adventure around the world. Join the journey by reading his travelogue, exploring the topics inside the Compendium, or perusing the Snapshots gallery.

Trek Hound - a web site for independent travelers. Here you will find information on travel literature, movies, travel tips, budget saving ideas, chronicles of past trips, food and lodging reviews, information on pet travel and much more.

Viator Travel Blog - The staff at Viator are passionate travelers. When they're not busy talking about their last trip, they're busy planning their next adventure. On Viator, they share their passion and inspire all of us to make that next trip.

Wanderlust and Lipstick - Wanderlust and Lipstick provides both the nervous newbie and the well-seasoned Wanderluster with all the tools needed to set out on a dream journey, whether to Paris, Peoria or Prague! Find travel stories to whet your appetite for adventures around the globe, read travel tips from experienced globetrotters, learn about Wanderlust and Lipstick-recommended travel gear, and salivate over the glorious photos in the WanderGallery submitted by travelers the world over.

Working Your Way Around the World - Between telecommuting, work visas and networking, it's perfectly possible to pick up and move to different parts of the world on a regular basis — and work along the way. We focus on jobs that you can be proud to put on your resume, from finding a job abroad to building a business of your own, we've got the resources you need.

Write Away! - Lauren Carter is an award-winning writer whose articles about trekking in Ecuador, searching out authentic tango in Buenos Aires, hiking the Matra Hills in Hungary, paddling Ontario's French River and discovering Toronto's West Queen West have appeared in National Geographic Traveler, Arthur Frommer's Budget Travel, the Toronto Star, and many more.

PART 4
The Top 25 Bucket List Goals

"One day your life will flash before your eyes. Make sure it's worth watching."

- The Bucket List

25 MOST POPULAR BUCKET LIST GOALS

What's on your bucket list?

With over three million bucket list goals on Bucketlist.org I have a pretty unique insight into what *a lot* of people want to accomplish in their lives. One of the biggest struggles that people face when creating their lists, is figuring out what they want to do in the first place. Whether you're going around the world or around your city, check out the list below of the top 25 goals from Bucketlist.org, how many people want to accomplish the goal and how many people have successfully achieved the goal.

What's the difference between dreams, goals, and reality? Goals are dreams with a plan, and realities are goals that have come to fruition. So take to time and live the life of your dreams.

How you can live the life of your dreams
It starts with a bucket list. The power of a bucket list is that it transcends countries, cultures, and stereotypes.

It is simply the first step in taking action on your dreams. And to be completely honest, at first I had some doubts about the whole idea of a bucket list. It seemed like something frivolous. But today I am fully converted to the idea, and I am very close to living my dreams 100% of the time.

Visualize your future.
The first step to living your dreams is visualizing your future. Take a moment to see where you'll be in 5, 10, 15 years. First, if your life continues on the current track you're on, and second, a more, dream scenario. Are you happy with what you see in scenario one, or could things be better? Now what makes the things in your dream scenario, well, so dreamy? Figuring out the difference between your projected reality and your dreams is really the beginning of a chasing your best life. The things you want and need to strive towards to be the best version of yourself, living the best life.

Find your balance.
When you envision the direction you want to go in, it's important to evaluate where you are at this present moment, in order to gain true perspective on your life. Of course the majority of people would like to drop everything, pack up and go on a year long vacation, but to be blunt, that's just not a feasible vocation to go after. A balance between responsibilities and your goals is crucial to find. It makes the journey to living your dreams actually attainable, small incremental changes create habits, which over some period of time, make huge impacts on your life. And ultimately finding this balance will help you eliminate excuses from holding you back in life.

Focus on things that matter.
Be true to what you want and who you are. Although being so interconnected is a powerful thing, it can also be increasingly distracting from the end goal. Use your bucket list as a guide to what matters most in life.

So you've set your goals, and you've begun to take the next steps to start crossing off your bucket list goals. But sometimes it's hard to stay driven and motivated. Take a look at successful people's habits because there is so much we can learn from them. Here are:

Five things successful goal setters (and achievers) do that you should too:

1. Wake Up Early
It may seem like a little bit of a no-brainer, but studies have shown that waking up early (I'm talking 5am) will make you more proactive and more productive. I'll admit, I love sleeping, it's wonderful, but in the long run I know checking off one of those bucket list items will feel so much better than hitting the snooze button for five more minutes of sleep.

2. Map out Your Day
I'm a big believer of lists: to-do lists, daily tasks, and, of course, life lists. If you don't think you have time to do something, scheduling your day, or even your week, will make you more productive.

3. Watch one hour Less of TV a Day
Again, TV is awesome, but is it really a good use of time? If you're finding that you're running low on time, but still manage to watch the entire season of *House of Cards* in one

sitting, try cutting down your TV time, at least a little bit, and put it toward achieving a goal.

4. Set Specific Goals and Prioritize Them
SMART goal setting works, and additionally, by prioritizing what you want to accomplish, it will make sure you won't feel overwhelmed. A lot of people feel discouraged from a failure or setback, so prioritizing and working your goals into your daily routine will help keep you on track.

5. Exercise/Meditate
Finally, a common thread of successful goal setters is that they make time to exercise and/or meditate. Personal development and maintaining a well-balanced lifestyle will alleviate stress and help put the big things into perspective.

Without further adieu, here are the top 25 bucket list goals from Bucketlist.org.

SEE THE NORTHERN LIGHTS
(Aurora Borealis)

10,194 people have this goal on their bucket list
562 have achieved this goal

"They were the most beautiful thing I've ever seen... ever! It was in Lapland, Finland. I went near a forest where there were no lights at all. I could see the stars like I've never seen them before - I could even see satellites. I was already really amazed by the sky, but when the northern lights appeared it was even more amazing. It's like if someone was painting the sky in green, the lights were moving and changing colors from green to purple and red. It probably lasted for half an hour and it was the only time I saw them. I would love to see them again I'm sure it will be as amazing as the first time and different.[22]"

---

[22] http://bucketlist.org/discover/see-the-northern-lights/#.VRjZdtx331o

See the Northern Lights
(Aurora Borealis)

The Northern Lights, or Aurora Borealis, are a natural light display caused by the collision of the solar wind and magnetosphere-charged particles with the high altitude atmosphere. While the Northern Lights obviously happen in northern latitudes, there is a southern counterpart, the Aurora Australis, though they aren't as well known or popular. These particles seem to paint the sky in waving, unearthly colors, usually greens, blues, or reds and are extremely beautiful and enchanting.

Seeing the Northern Lights should be on your bucket list because of their unique and unusual nature. Because they only appear at high latitudes, many of us have never seen them. They seem strange and magical and shouldn't be overlooked, it's no wonder they are the number one most popular goal on the site.

In order to see the Northern Lights, you'll need to travel to Alaska, northern parts of Canada, the southern half of Greenland, Iceland, Northern Norway, Sweden or Finland, as well as the western half of the Russian north. It's also possible to see the lights from southern Scandinavia, north-central United States, and sometimes Scotland, though it's unlikely, and you would want to make a special trip there to see the Lights.

The best likelihood of seeing the Northern Lights is between late September and Late March from about 6 pm to 4 am, though, since these high-latitude areas are dark most of the day during this time, it's possible to see the Lights outside of this window. Just check the weather, as you'll need a clear sky to view them. For those of us in North America, the closest places to view the lights are Yellowknife, Canada, and Fairbanks, Alaska, USA, otherwise, Northern Scandinavia have spectacular displays of dancing light.

VISIT A VOLCANO

11,684 people have this goal on their bucket list
2302 have achieved this goal

"Italy (June 2013) Climbed a volcano after exploring Pompeii. Pretty tough on the way up but definitely worth the views from the top. Feel so privileged to have been able to do it in good company and youth.[23]"

24

---

[23] http://bucketlist.org/discover/visit-a-volcano/

Visit a Volcano

Volcanoes are some of the most destructive natural phenomenon on earth. They are a rupture on the earth's crust that allows hot lava, volcanic ash, and gases to escape from below the earth's surface. Volcanoes are found where tectonic plates meet and where there is a stretching and thinning of the crust. All over earth, both on land and on the sea floor, there are active and extinct volcanoes. The most active volcanoes on earth are Kīlauea in Hawaii, Mount Etna and Stromboli in the Mediterranean, and Mount Yasuar on the South Pacific Island of Vanatu.

Visiting a volcano should be on your bucket list because it's uncommon in daily life, it can be educational, and a little adrenaline inducing. Most people want to look something this huge, powerful, and destructive right in the face. And it's also difficult to understand how they work, so being close you can start to have a sense of understanding.

Mount Vesuvius in Italy, Mount Fuji in Japan, Mount Bromo in Indonesia, and Kīlauea in Hawaii are some of the most popular and beautiful volcanoes to visit. While all of these volcanoes have their beauty and benefits, Kīlauea in Hawaii might be the best to visit. It's been actively erupting since the early 1980s and is continuously changing because of the hardening lava. While this sounds scary, especially after the massive eruptions we all know about Vesuvius and Fuji, the lava actually flows slowly, making it one of the safest active volcanoes in the world. It's an added benefit to seeing a volcano in action as well as capturing the beautiful surroundings nearby.

24

RIDE IN A HOT AIR BALLOON

12,167 people have this goal on their bucket list
609 have achieved this goal

"Saw the sun rise over the Nile at Luxor from a hot air balloon while on holiday with my mum. Simply, magical[25]*"*

---

[25] http://bucketlist.org/discover/RIDE-A-HOT-AIR-BALLOON/

Ride in a Hot Air Balloon

Hot air balloons are the oldest successful human-carrying flight technology. These balloons are actually called an envelope and contain heated air to carry a whicker basket. The heated air inside the envelope makes it buoyant, allowing the balloon, and its passengers to float above the cooler, denser air around them.

Riding in a hot air balloon should be on your bucket list because of its novelty and serenity. The balloon allows you to slowly float, rather than flying quickly like in a plane, and view the world around you from up high. We all want to experience the sensation of floating and also seeing gorgeous surroundings. It's only natural for us all to want to view the world in this way.

Many companies around the world offer rides. Some of the best locations are the Loire Valley, France; Serengeti National Park, Tanzania; Napa Valley, California, USA; Cappadocia, Turkey; Istria, Croatia; Gstaad, Switzerland; Albuquerque, New Mexico, USA; and the Yarra Valley, Australia. Rides typically last about an hour and are usually between $100-$250, depending on where you are and what you want to do. But if you can't make it to one of these more exotic locations, many places in less popular areas offer slightly cheaper rides if you're looking to just experience floating above the earth.

VISIT NIAGARA FALLS

10659 people have this goal on their bucket list
2674 have achieved this goal

"We visited Niagara Falls on 20th July 2014 (Canada side). Awesome experience, it was. We took the Hornblower cruise near the falls. It was thrilling to be so near the thunderous falls. Lifetime experience.[26]"

---

[26] http://bucketlist.org/discover/visit-niagara-falls/

Visit Niagara Falls

Niagara Falls is the name of three waterfalls that span the border between Canada and the United States between New York State and Ontario. The three falls are the Horseshoe Falls, the American Falls, and the Bridal Veil Falls. The Horseshoe Falls lay mostly on the Canadian side and are the most recognizable part of Niagara Falls. The closest major cities to the falls are Buffalo, NY, 17 miles, and Toronto, Ontario, 75 miles. The falls get their fame from being the largest waterfall in North America, and depositing the most water of any waterfall in the world.

Niagara Falls should be on your bucket list because of these statistics, but also because of their astounding beauty. The falls straddle two countries and two Great Lakes, and are surrounded by many sites and attractions, such as the Maid of the Mist, a boat ride that takes you near the Falls; Niagara Falls State Park in New York; and a large tourist area in Niagara Falls, Canada. And while it's not officially on a World Wonder list, it's definitely among some of the top natural sites in the world, along with the Grand Canyon, Mount Kilimanjaro, and the Great Barrier Reef.

To visit the falls, you can fly into Toronto or Buffalo Niagara airports, though Buffalo is much closer than Toronto. Either place you fly to, it's easiest to rent a car, unless you book a tour, as public transportation isn't always available.
While both sides, the American and Canadian, have their benefits, the Canadian side has a better view, where you are looking across at the falls, whereas on the American side you are right near the Niagara River and can better feel their power.

Try to visit both sides of the falls, so don't forget your passport! Experience the neon lights, and tourist attractions of Clifton Hill on the Canadian side, and the parks of the American. Visiting the falls is free, but if you want to get really close to the falls, the Maid of the Mist is $17 and leaves from the American side.

GO TO A DRIVE IN MOVIE

813 people have this goal on their bucket list
237 have achieved this goal

"Have always loved the idea of eating greasy fries and watered down coke whilst sitting in my car in front of a massive movie screen. I must say I blame it mostly on Grease and their trip to the drive-in.[27]*"*

---

[27] http://bucketlist.org/discover/go-to-a-drive-in-movie/

Go to a Drive-in Movie

A drive-in movie theatre is an outdoor cinema that uses a projector to show the movie on a large screen and has a large parking area for viewing. People can either stay in their cars to watch the movie, listening to the audio through the car radio, or sit outside on chairs or a grassy area closer to the screen and listen through evenly spaced speakers. Drive-in theatres were very popular in the 1960s in the U.S. but have died down in popularity and frequency since the '80s.

A drive-in theatre should be on your bucket list because they are a fun spin on the regular movie theatre. You can bring your own food, hang out in your car or bring lawn chairs, and make a party out of it. It's nice to sit where you want, not be crowded in uncomfortable movie seats, and just be outside. Some of the most fun is that movies usually start late, after the sun goes down in summer, so you're out with friends, watching good movies, and having a fun time.

To accomplish this, research if a drive-in is close to you. In North America, you might not have to drive very far to find one, especially in summer. If it is far away, make a road trip out of it. Research the movies, bring some friends, and make it an event. It's definitely a fun alternative to watching in a theatre or in your home. You'll be hooked!

SWIM WITH DOLPHINS

21,052 people have this goal on their bucket list
3329 have achieved this goal

"It was actually one of the most unforgettable experiences of my life! They're amazing creatures if you haven't swam with dolphins go do it![28]"

---

[28] http://bucketlist.org/discover/swim-with-dolphins/

Swim with Dolphins

Swimming with Dolphins has quickly become a popular activity for many travelers. In typical dolphinariums (dolphin aquariums), which can be deep pools, ponds, or specially marked ocean areas, swimmers interact in various ways with the dolphins. In some places, swimmers can hold onto the dolphin's fin as it swims, but more recently this isn't allowed. Typically, swimmers are shown how to be a trainer, giving commands to the dolphins and watching them perform. But there is also controversy about the treatment of dolphins in dolphinariums, so we might see a big change in the future.

This is on many people's bucket lists because dolphins are beautiful, majestic, and intelligent animals. It's exciting to be in their vicinity, and they are often playful and fun to interact with. The average person very rarely sees dolphins, so getting an up-close glance at them is a real treat. Because many dolphinariums mistreat the dolphins, an alternative to this might be viewing dolphins in the wild on a boat, or, if you're really brave, cage diving with sharks.

Many countries don't allow swimming with dolphins because of this mistreatment. It's important to do your research before deciding where to interact with dolphins because while it may be fun and exciting to swim with them, it's not worth it to keep them in constant harm for our enjoyment. If you're unsure how the dolphins are treated, try something different, like diving with sharks! Most of the time, you would be out in the open ocean with wild and untrained sharks that are just lured to your area with food. You still get an up-close-and-personal view of an animal, but this time without the guilt of the animal being mistreated for your enjoyment. But like any animal activity, always be informed on what happens behind the scenes.

DO EPIC SHIT

JUMP IN A POOL FULLY CLOTHED

139 people have this goal on their bucket list
53 have achieved this goal

"My two friends and I decided to do this one night. Hilarious. I couldn't move my clothes were so heavy.[29]"

---

[29] http://bucketlist.org/discover/jump-in-a-pool-fully-clothed/#.VSm7jdx331o

135

Jump in a pool fully clothed

Sometimes bucket list items are about letting yourself go, to be free to do what you want. And sometimes that's jumping in a pool fully clothed. Jumping in a pool fully clothed is pretty self-explanatory. Basically, just keep your clothes on and hop on in. A variation on this could be going in an ocean, lake or river fully clothed. This can be fun in the summer when it's really hot and you just need to immediately cool off, or somebody pushes you into the pool as a joke.

This should be on your bucket list because it's something you wouldn't normally do. It's fun, a little silly, and sort of breaks the rules. Sometimes we get so caught up in trying to be adults or acting mature that we forget to have fun and let loose. This is the epitome of acting like a kid and having fun.

Actually accomplishing this task takes barely anything. All you need is a pool, or any body of water, really. It's fun to have a bunch of friends to share in the experience, so get a big group, throw on some clothes you don't care about getting wet, check your pockets for electronics, and take the plunge. Hopefully the water's warm!

VISIT DISNEYLAND

5762 people have this goal on their bucket list
4054 have achieved this goal

"One of the best journeys in my life. I found out that magic never ends even though you grew up.[30] "

Visit Disneyland

They say Disney parks are the happiest places on Earth. They have rides, food, games, shows, and an awesome atmosphere that makes everyone feel like a kid again. Not only is it a fun amusement park, you can also see characters from your favorite movies and shows, explore their different lands, and just embrace the kid in you. Disney is such a big franchise that everyone knows it, and everyone enjoys it on some levels. And there are so many parks that there seems to be something for everyone. There are resorts in Florida and California in the USA, plus Tokyo, Paris, Hong Kong, and Shanghai, with multiple parks, countless hotels, and other venues in each location.

Disney parks are among the most well-known in the world, and because of Disney's massive empire, are extremely popular to visit. People want to visit as children to see their favorite characters and enjoy the great rides and shows, and they want to visit as adults to relive those feelings and possibly see their children feel the same way. Disney parks continue to be on people's bucket lists because of this child-like quality, and the novelty of visiting a famous attraction.

Visiting any Disneyland around the world can be expensive, not even including transportation there. Do your research to find deals on park admission, hotels and getting there. There are discounts for groups, if you're staying at a Disney hotel, and if you're part of some organizations, like AAA in the U.S., and if you go to multiple parks or stay for multiple days. To make sure you don't break the bank, definitely plan ahead for these discounts and try to go far away from holidays as hotel prices skyrocket. But once you're there, just enjoy! Realize it's not cheap, and try to do as much as possible so you experience everything.

BUNGEE JUMP

14,307 people have this goal on their bucket list
1145 have achieved this goal

"I FINALLY DID IT! After a few days of pestering my friends to go along with me, a total of 7 of us took a 2 hours drive from Vancouver to Whistler Bungee for this big thing. The staffs were really friendly and professional, and the jump went on really fast and smooth. The adrenaline rush was crazy - scary indeed during the free fall but hanging in the air looking through the beautiful scenery surrounding? AMAZING. You'll never regret, trust me![31] "

---

[31] http://bucketlist.org/discover/bungee-jump/#.VSm9qtx331o

Bungee Jump

Bungee Jumping involves a tall structure that a person jumps off of while being connected by a long elastic cord. It's possible to bungee off of a bridge, building, crane, or even a hot air balloon or helicopter. As the person jumps, the cord stretches and the jumper flies upward as the cord recoils. The person bounces a little at the end before coming to a rest and then being helped down. Organized commercial bungee jumping started in New Zealand in 1986 at the Greenhithe Bridge in Auckland.

Bungee jumping should be on your bucket list because it's one of the most adrenaline-inducing activities in the world. You experience a free fall that might take your breath away, the feeling of weightlessness, and the fear that comes along with it all. And really, the purpose of a bucket list is to do things you wouldn't normally do, and jumping off of something very big is one of those things!

Of course, the bungee capital of the world is in New Zealand at The Nevis in Queenstown, but other amazing sites are Victoria Falls Bridge at the border of Zimbabwe and Zambia; Verzasca Dam, Ticino, Switzerland; Macau Tower, China; Extremo Park, Monteverde, Costa Rica; and Europabrücke, Innsbruck, Austria. But if you can't make it to any of these places, bungees can be found in many major cities all over the world. Make sure to bring your courage!

GO ON A CRUISE

12,553 people have this goal on their bucket list
3892 have achieved this goal

"Went on Royal Caribbean's Allure of the Seas for a week, it was AMAZING, it was the DreamWorks experience so, my daughter loved it as well. Visited Jamaica, Labadie and Cozumel, will definitely do it again in a heart beat.[32]"

---

[32] http://bucketlist.org/discover/GO-ON-A-CRUISE/#.VSm-idx331o

Go on a Cruise

A cruise is anywhere from 2-14 days spent traveling on a large cruise liner. These ships are usually massive, carrying thousands of people and having everything from many concert halls and arenas, to many pools, spas, restaurants, and gyms. They are like floating cities that can transport people from one place to another in comfort.

A cruise should be on your bucket list because it's a form of travel in itself that is uncommon. It's a luxury to go to sleep at night, in the same bed, and wake up in a new port, or relax by the pool as you're transported across the ocean. You have many dining options, so you will never be hungry, and can enjoy the sun while traveling, before going ashore to shop and visit the locals.

Taking a cruise can be expensive, as you're paying for a room, all food, and your transportation to the port and back. But, if you keep an eye on deals, you can find a great rate that won't break the bank. You'll be able to relax, venture on land when you want, and come back refreshed instead of jet-lagged from flying and transporting yourself around. And it is definitely worth a little extra money for the experience.

SEE A CIRQUE DU SOLEIL SHOW

7568 people have this goal on their bucket list
2964 have achieved this goal

"Saw 'Mystere' at Treasure Island, Las Vegas while on honeymoon. Most magical show I've ever seen.[33]"

---

[33] http://bucketlist.org/discover/see-a-cirque-de-soleil-show/#.VSm_s9x331o

See a Cirque du Soleil show

Cirque du Soleil is a Canadian company that describes itself as "a dramatic mix of circus arts and street entertainment." It's an amazing show of acrobatics and stunts executed by talented performers. There are many types of shows with different themes that are performed at different venues around the world, most notably Las Vegas, with many shows at many resorts, and at many Disney parks around the world.

Cirque du Soleil should be on your bucket list because it's an amazing and mind-bending show that should be seen at least once. It's amazing to see these performers seemingly do the impossible. You'll be transported to another world.

Cirque du Soleil often tours, so make sure to check venues near you to see if they might be coming there. If not, try to make it to Las Vegas to take your pick from the different shows, or visit a Disney park (you might be able to kill two birds with one stone on that one). Tickets can be pretty expensive, depending on where you are, but it's definitely worth it for the show. Then just sit back and be mesmerized by the talent.

VISIT THE WHITE HOUSE

8355 people have this goal on their bucket list
1912 have achieved this goal

"Well, it was only outside the white house but I got to tour around the Capital.[34]"

---

[34] http://bucketlist.org/discover/visit-the-white-house/#.VSnBCNx331o

Visit the White House

The White House is the official workplace and residence for the United States President. It's in Washington, D.C. on Pennsylvania Avenue and is a major attraction in the city, along with many famous monuments and government buildings.

This is on most people's bucket list because it is one of the most recognizable buildings in the world, or at least most people have heard of the White House. It's very restricted, making it exciting to catch a glimpse of it, and be near the workplace of one of the most powerful people in the world.

Seeing the White House is easy. You can walk down Pennsylvania Avenue to view it through a fence, though it is set back, with a massive lawn in between. Guards are everywhere, so make sure not to try anything silly. It's extremely difficult to actually enter the White House, made only on special pre-arranged tours approved by Congressional representatives in your area or at embassies in Washington for foreign nationals. But to go on these tours, you go through intensive background checks that could take a very long time. So start writing to your Congressman or talking to your embassy!

RIDE AN ELEPHANT

12,548 people have this goal on their bucket list
2452 have achieved this goal

"Beautiful and majestic...They're just such amazing animals.[35]"

---

[35] http://bucketlist.org/discover/RIDE-AN-ELEPHANT/

Ride an Elephant

Elephant riding has been a tradition in India for centuries and has spread to many other places in Africa and Southeast Asia. And while it seems like a fun form of transport, the elephants actually undergo torture during training. Recently, many major companies are taking a stand against elephant riding because of the cruel measures that go into their training.

Elephant riding is on many people's bucket lists because elephants are massive and majestic creatures that most of us rarely come in contact with. Because we see movies and pictures of others riding elephants, it has become a must on bucket lists, as we all want to experience that contact with them, though we don't always know what goes on behind the scenes to make the elephants tame to ride.

Instead of riding elephants, you can visit an elephant sanctuary, like the most famous one, Elephant Nature Park, in Thailand. At the park you can interact with elephants much more than if you were riding them, by volunteering to prepare their food, cleaning the elephants and the area they live, and constructing mud pits and other necessities for the elephants. You'll also learn about elephants in depth, about their families, their daily lives, how they have been mistreated, and the future of their population in Thailand. This is definitely a better way to go, as you'll be spending more time with elephants and learning about them as wild animals, not just a mode of transportation.

LEARN A NEW LANGUAGE

12,575 people have this goal on their bucket list
1555 have achieved this goal

"This was my goal for the past 2 years. And I completed it. I learned Spanish. Grammar was the toughest to me (as always).[36]"

---

[36] http://bucketlist.org/discover/learn-a-new-language/#.VSnDLtx331o

Learn a New Language

Learning a new language is a great way to continue to learn or just gain a new skill. Knowing another language can make you more creative, will boost your self-esteem, gives you a step up when applying for a job, improves cognitive power, and obviously helps with communication skills in all the languages you know.

Learning a new language should be on your bucket list because, especially in North America, we tend to only know English, so there's a huge drawback when traveling and a language barrier is present. Learning a second – or third language – is key in better communication when abroad and to understand the world around us a little more. It's also becoming much more popular and cool because it's a great skill to have. And who doesn't want to show off how much we know?

To learn a new language, you need to first pick a language, though that's obvious. Some of the most common languages to learn, in North America, are French, Spanish, and German, but some of the most widely spoken languages in the world are Chinese, Arabic, and Russian. So what will you pick? Once you've decided, start collecting resources, dictionaries, books, movies, and podcasts in the language, and look for classes or a language exchange partner. You'll have to really immerse yourself in the language if you want to learn it quickly. Maybe even plan a trip to boost your knowledge of the language and culture.

THROW A DART AT A MAP AND TRAVEL TO WHERE IT LANDS

10,540 people have this goal on their bucket list
29 have achieved this goal

"The spontaneity would be so exciting![37]"

---

[37] http://bucketlist.org/i/nLZ1/#.VSnEndx331o

Throw a Dart at a Map and Travel to where it Lands

Throwing a dart at a map is a really fun and adventurous way to pick where you should travel next. Whether you've traveled a lot and just want to do something spontaneous, or haven't traveled much but can't decide where to go, it's a silly way to let the "universe" decide where you should go.

This is on a many people's bucket lists because of the novelty and spontaneity it has. To let a dart make a big decision takes a little of the pressure off, and allows us to sit back and enjoy the ride that is travel. If you've ever wanted to travel, and just can't decide where, or have never traveled on a whim, this should definitely be on your list, too.

While the act of throwing the dart itself is pretty easy, the paying for the travel is the difficult part. You could do it one of two ways. Start saving money, and when you have a sufficient amount, let the dart tell you where to travel, or throw the dart and save up according to the destination. I would go with the first one because it's a little more exciting and immediate if you can start booking travel with the money you saved right after finding out where to go.

TAKE A PICTURE EVERY DAY FOR A YEAR

2451 people have this goal on their bucket list
521 have achieved this goal

"I wanted to document how much I changed in one year's time. It's weird how you can actually notice a difference.[38]"

---

[38] http://bucketlist.org/i/nMcN/

Take a Picture Every day for a Year

Taking a picture every day for a year can either be of you or of a specific location. The reason behind it is to see what changes during that year because it's hard for us to see the changes while we're in the moment. It's amazing to look back and see how you've changed or how the scenery has changed around you. And it's also a great keepsake, much like a journal, so you can look back and remember those times.

This should be on your bucket list because we often talk about how life is too short and that we need to do more things during our time. This is a great way to be reminded to always remember the little things. Because we can't possibly remember every day, taking a photo captures just a glimpse of our lives and, put side by side with other photos, is a way to be more present during days of your life.

Because this project takes a year, you'll need to be dedicated to doing it *every day*. Luckily, the daily task only takes a few seconds. First, pick where you want to take the picture. If it's of a specific location, you'll obviously need to make sure you are at that location for a year, or, possibly, make arrangements for someone to help if you're away. If it's of yourself, you have a little more leeway, but you'll still want to keep it consistent, so if you can be in the same location, it's much better. Then just set an alarm on your phone for the same time each day. Maybe do it right in the morning, or right before you leave the house for the day. By setting a reminder you'll keep the conditions the same and will never forget. Now just get a camera, your phone, or computer, and start. Just remember why you're doing it, and you'll be motivated to stick it out the whole year. You'll be surprised to see the change over the year. You can even piece all the photos together using an app and make a video of the progression of your project.

UNPLUG FOR 48 HOURS

9,654 people have this goal on their bucket list
2452 have achieved this goal

"You think this would be an easy goal, but it was challenging not to pick up my phone every time I got bored.[39]*"*

---

[39] http://bucketlist.org/i/nMgA/#.VSq1Pdx331o

"Unplug" for 48 hours

Unplugging for 48 hours is definitely a new bucket list item. Because we are so connected to our phones, computers, and television, we can sometimes get lost in all of the technology. This item is relatively easy, as you just have to *not* do something – but you'd be surprised at how challenging it can be. You can't be on your phone, computer, listen to music, watch TV, or really be around any sort of technology for 48 hours.

This should be on your bucket list because we all need a little time away from the technology that has overwhelmed us. And while we all love the instant gratification of Googling directions or questions we want answered, it definitely makes our brain work a different way when that's not possible. To unplug means you have to find entertainment elsewhere and might need to rely more on yourself and other people rather than the Internet. Even if you hate being unplugged, you'll look at technology a little differently afterwards and possibly appreciate what you have a little more.

It seems easy to unplug, but it can be a very long 48 hours if you aren't prepared. The easiest way is to get a group of people to participate as well, that way you aren't isolating yourself, making the task even more daunting. With a group, you can find tasks to do that don't have to do with technology. You can go camping, cook for a big group, or just play board games you might have played when you were younger (or have never played!). The key is to keep busy, and be far enough away from your phone or computer so that you aren't tempted. You'll be surprised how easy it is to stay away when you aren't thinking about it.

FLOAT IN THE DEAD SEA

10,873 people have this goal on their bucket list
534 have achieved this goal

"Awesome experience and I got a mud mask! Went with Escape Travels in December 2014 over Qatar National Day.[40]"

---

[40] http://bucketlist.org/discover/float-in-the-dead-sea/#.VSq3UNx331o

Float in the Dead Sea

The Dead Sea is a salt lake bordering Jordan, Palestine, and Israel. It is the world's saltiest body of water at 9.6 times saltier than the ocean. It's called the Dead Sea because animals and plants cannot live in the harsh salt water. Many people flock to the Dead Sea for its health benefits, with many spa resorts surrounding it, and also because the salt makes swimming more like floating.

This should be on your bucket list because it's a unique experience where this type of floating can't be found elsewhere in the world. It also has many health benefits because of its saltiness and its low elevation - the lowest on earth. It's also in a beautiful part of the world that needs to be experienced separate from the Dead Sea.

To accomplish this you'll need to travel to Jordan or Israel. Probably the most popular place to visit the Dead Sea is Mineral Beach in Israel. There's a huge mud pit to roll around in, to benefit your skin, of course, as well as natural Jacuzzis and a freshwater pool if you get sick of the salt. You can rent a towel, locker, and get a health treatment if you want as well as use showers, eat in the cafeteria, and sunbathe on a beach less pebbly than other Dead Sea beaches. Mineral Beach is closest to Jerusalem, so it's perfect for a day trip.

VISIT EVERY CONTINENT IN THE WORLD

9851 people have this goal on their bucket list
39 have achieved this goal

"Done: Europe, North America, Asia, Africa. Remaining: South America, Oceania, Antarctic.[41] "

---

[41] http://bucketlist.org/discover/VISIT-every-continent-in-the-world/#.VSq4ztx331o

Visit Every Continent in the World

Visiting every continent in the world would mean you are well-traveled, have experienced many things, and have lived a full and active life. People often visit every continent in the world over many years and several trips, though a few very adventurous and motivated travelers get them all in one go. With the ever-growing technology today, it's easier than ever to travel and reach all corners of the globe.

This should be on your bucket list for all of those important reasons. Visiting so many diverse people and cultures means you have a better understanding of the world and have greater knowledge than many people around you. If you've traveled to every continent, you've experienced a wide variety of cultures and people and will definitely be a better person for it.

To accomplish this, you'll basically have to start traveling! Start setting goals for when you will accomplish each continent and start saving. Because you'll have to fly far from home, the airfare can be pretty drastic, but if you plan right, you'll be able to accomplish it easily in your lifetime. Just stay motivated, and stay excited to travel. If possible, travel to a few continents at a time, as it might be cheaper to fly from place to place rather than continuous round trips from your home. But most importantly, start now planning now.

RIDE IN A GONDOLA IN VENICE ITALY

8787 people have this goal on their bucket list
1003 have achieved this goal

"Did it and yes it is the total cliché of clichés except for our gondolier...he was really a race boat driver so the slow and lazy pace of a gondola was difficult for him to amuse himself...but he did try.[42]"

---

[42] http://bucketlist.org/discover/ride-a-gondola-in-venice-italy/#.VSrBGNx331o

Ride in a Gondola in Venice, Italy

Venice is made up of many small waterways and rivers, making boats the easiest way to get around. Gondolas are long, flat-bottomed boats that are propelled by a gondolier, who pushes the boat with a long pole, using the bottom of the canal for leverage. Gondolas were the most common watercraft in Venice for centuries, but small motorboats and large ferries are more commonly used now, making gondolas an iconic and special adventure.

Riding on a gondola in Venice should be on your bucket list because it's romantic, exciting, and a departure from the norm. The gondolier might sing to you or your group, and it will be a pleasant ride through the canals of Venice, an awesome way to see the city.

To accomplish this, you'll obviously have to travel to Venice. It's not the cheapest city in the world, so definitely save up. And make sure to budget for the gondola ride, as they can be pretty expensive. Then just find an unoccupied boat and you're off! Relax and float on the canal, watching the city go by from a different angle.

GO TO THE TOP OF THE EIFFEL TOWER

7859 people have this goal on their bucket list
2074 have achieved this goal

"Cannot say more than 'I loved it.' The view at this height is breathtaking. But I have to admit, I liked the view from the Arc de Triomphe a little bit more. Without the Eiffel Tower as landmark of this beautiful city would be missing something.[43]"

---

[43] http://bucketlist.org/discover/go-to-the-top-of-the-eiffel-tower/#.VSrBuNx331o

Go to the Top of the Eiffel Tower

The Eiffel Tower in Paris is one of the most distinctive landmarks in the world. Everyone knows what it is, and everyone knows it's in Paris. And most people want to go to the top. It is 324 meters high, about the same as an 81-story building and the tallest structure in Paris. To get to the top, passengers can either ride one of two elevators to the first and second levels, or walk. And it is possible to go all the way to the top with a special ticket.

This should be on your bucket list because it's an amazing experience to view Paris from the Eiffel Tower. Because Paris keeps its buildings low, there is always a view over the city and you can see all around, even glimpsing some other famous landmarks like the Arc de Triomphe and Sacre Coeur. There is also something magical about the Eiffel Tower that makes it very exciting to ascend.

It's a good idea to buy tickets online in advance because lines can get very crazy and you'll spend most of the day standing around. You can even book a specific time of day to visit that will cut down your wait even more, so just be on time! After waiting in line, just ride to the top and enjoy the view.

VISIT A CASTLE

7314 people have this goal on their bucket list
2255 have achieved this goal

"I'm not sure if I've been to more castles, but one I remember clearly was visiting Boldt Castle in Alexandria Bay, a few years back. Such a beautiful site, I recommend everyone to view the tour. It's best during the summer.[44]"

---

[44] http://bucketlist.org/discover/visit-a-castle/#.VSrCSdx331o

Visit a Castle

Castles are some of the oldest man-made structures that are extremely beautiful and interesting to visit. And especially for North Americans, they are very rare to see, so it adds another level of historical mystery. Castles differ around the world, but we mostly think of medieval fortresses where kings ruled and knights fought.

Most people want to visit a castle because they like the history and the stories behind them. Battles might have been fought there, and princes may have turned into kings. It's also interesting to see the different architecture, how people built things and lived in a time we can barely understand, and try to imagine what it was like. It's definitely a draw for many people.

There are hundreds of castles around the world to choose from, but if you want to visit some medieval castles, the United Kingdom is packed full of them with the most famous ones being Edinburgh Castle, Urquhart Castle, Caernarfon Castle, Arundel Castle, Alnwick Castle, and Windsor Castle, just to name a few. Not only are these amazingly well-maintained, but they are also in relatively close proximity, so you can hit a lot of them in one trip.

WALK BEHIND A WATERFALL

6130 people have this goal on their bucket list
801 have achieved this goal

"As the remnants of Hurricane Ernesto chased us across the Yucatan in Mexico, we visited Misol-Ha. Because of the heavy rains you couldn't trek all the way across behind the waterfall, but you could go pretty far. The power of the water was intense and exhilarating.[45]"

---

[45] http://bucketlist.org/i/nMeS/#.VSrHk9x331o

Walk Behind a Waterfall

A waterfall is a beautiful work of nature. They can be very big, like Niagara Falls, or very small at your local creek. We mostly look at them from the front and so we always wonder what they're like from the back, if there is some secret cave or just the rock.

Because of this mystery, there's no wonder many people have this on their bucket list. We want to see things from a different angle and we want to experience what it's like on the other side. It is amazing to see the water falling all around you and hear and feel the water's power when it's so close.

Depending on where you live, this might not be so difficult. There are plenty of small waterfalls that you can sneak behind, or if you're looking for something more substantial, try the Maid of the Mist at Niagara Falls while you're crossing that off your list. Two in one!

SEE THE GRAND CANYON

9387 people have this goal on their bucket list
2160 have achieved this goal

"Completed this last year, when I went to Vegas. It truly was amazing and a must see in your lifetime. Me and my friend had booked this trip before we went out, a lot of the trips last the whole day, we didn't want on that took up our whole day. I booked an aeroplane trip around the canyon, luckily for us I had a window seat and my friend had a seat opposite the door so our views weren't blocked. If I did it again I would get a helicopter around the canyon, with the opportunity to step foot, on this natural beauty. Absolutely amazing and a must do for anyone going to Vegas. Worth the time and effort.[46]"

---

[46] http://bucketlist.org/discover/see-the-grand-canyon/#.VSrJHNx331o

See the Grand Canyon

The Grand Canyon is a steep-sided canyon carved by the Colorado River in Arizona, USA. It is 277 miles long, 18 miles wide, and is over a mile deep, making it one of the world's largest canyons. It is also considered one of the Seven Natural Wonders of the World. It's amazing to view the canyon, seeing all of the rock striations and the vast expanse.

This should be on your bucket list because it's a vast and amazing sight. It's difficult to comprehend just how large it is, and how something like this could form. It's a popular place to visit and almost a rite of passage, at least for most people in North America, because everyone wants to view it.

To visit the Grand Canyon, you can fly into either Las Vegas or Phoenix, and drive roughly five hours from either to where you can stay in many local hotels. Tours also leave from both cities and do day trips. Travel during the winter, when prices will be lower and crowds will be thinner, and make sure to schedule enough time to enter the park - there's a fee - and to spend time wandering around without rushing.

GO ROCK CLIMBING

7307 people have this goal on their bucket list
1979 have achieved this goal

"This was a tough one... at first. It was mentally challenging just as much as physically. Just when you think you can't go any higher because you're scared, you figure it out and make it work. Great for team building and personal development. Definitely hooked on rock climbing and will be doing this again and again and again![47]"

---

[47] http://bucketlist.org/discover/go-rock-climbing/#.VSrJ4dx331o

Go Rock Climbing

Rock climbing is the act of, well, climbing rocks! It's a great form of exercise and is exhilarating, and adrenaline inducing. Usually, people climb rocks on a pre-defined route with the help of a harness and spotters in case of falls. Popular rock climbing destinations include Grand Teton National Park in Wyoming, USA; Mount Temple, Banff National Park, Canada; Agulha do Diablo, Brazil; Kalymnos Island, Greece; and Mount Roraima, Venezuela.

Rock climbing should be on your bucket list because it's a great way to stay in shape, a fun exercise, and an adrenaline rush. You can climb in beautiful locations and find spectacular views along the way.

To accomplish this, you'll need to start practicing. You should be in pretty good shape with a good amount of both arm and leg strength so you don't burn out on your first climb. Once you are in shape, trying an indoor climb will help you adjust to the stress of climbing, while still being in a more secure environment. Once confident, you should find groups or tours that organize climbs in your area, or in a place you've always wanted to climb. By the time you reach this stage, you'll be accustomed to the rigorous work of climbing and will be able to enjoy where you are, and the excitement about the new climbs.

Those were the top 25 bucket list ideas from Bucketlist.org. If you're looking for even more inspiration, take a look at Bucketlist's ideas page, choked full of fresh ideas from over 200,000 members on the site.

PART 5
Feeling Inspired – Let's take it up a notch

"I've missed more than 9000 shots in my career. I've lost almost 300 games. 26 times I've been trusted to take the game winning shot and missed. I've failed over and over and over again in my life. And that is why I succeed."

–Michael Jordan

MIKE HORST – A BUCKET LIST HERO

Climbing Mount Everest

I think it's in my blood to share inspirational stories. I just can't help it. When I read what these incredible people – who really are just like me and you – are doing and achieving, it makes me want to accomplish items off my bucket list more than ever. And this is one of the *top* successes I've ever heard.

Climbing Mt. Everest

Climbing Everest encompasses everything bucket lists stand for. It's challenging, extreme, adventurous and above all, rewarding when you're able to stand on top of the world – literally. Mike Horst, has not only conquered the beast that is Everest but is the first person in the world to reach the summit of two 8,000 meter peaks in 24 hours – but more about that later. I had the pleasure of sitting down with Mike to talk about his incredibly inspiring life and I'm honored to share some of his remarkable stories.

Who is Mike Horst?

Growing up in the Puget Sound, it's no wonder that Mike fell in love with the mountains at a young age; to the west are the Olympic Mountains and to the East are the great Cascade Mountain Range. Now Mike is an accomplished climber calling Squamish, BC his home with his lovely and supportive wife Cassie and two-year-old son Cassidy. Mike works for a variety of guide services assisting climbers and dreamers alike to reach summits of the world's most beautiful mountains with Alpine Ascents International.

What was the first mountain you climbed?

"One of the first mountains I climbed – or tried to climb – was Mt. Constance out in the Olympic Mountains, and I was 8 years old and my dad and brother were up for it, and we started the steep hike and approach. We didn't make it anywhere near the summit because I was just so scared that I was crying and had to humbly ask my dad and brother if they'd be okay to not climb the mountain that day. And they realized they maybe had me bite off more than I could chew and we all went down. A couple years I went back as a young teenager with a couple of friends, and made it to the top. And I was really excited to, one have tried previously and not made it and come back years later and made it to the top. You can try a climb once, and learn a lot about it and come back more prepared and have success and an enjoyable time."

After that Mike got more and more into climbing, from the boy scouts, to climbing peaks with his high school friends. In university, Mike discovered that people could actually make money off of mountain guiding, and decided to pursue it as a career.

When people think bucket lists, Everest almost always comes to mind. Could you share a little more about your Everest experience. What was it like the first time you reached the highest point in the world?

"My first experience on Everest was a bit unique as I was hired to guide it. I had experience on other peaks in other 8000m peaks in the Himalayas and had been working as a mountain guide for around 10 years. I went there with Alpine Ascents International as one of their guides. And it was amazing, it was everything I hoped it was – a very busy place – but still really enjoyable. The terrain you climb through is absolutely spectacular, going up through the Khumbu icefall is exhilarating and beautiful. The summit ridge is absolutely spectacular, straddling the highest terrain on the planet between China and Nepal and climbing up as the sun rises, and as many teams progress up and down the mountain, is an experience I will cherish forever."

What is the biggest mistake you see people make when taking on Everest?

"It can be underestimated, even though it is a challenging goal, and people realize that, still folks will show up slightly under-prepared physically and or maybe they haven't done enough research as they should in terms of the appropriate gear to take with them or services to hire. Certainly the success rate on Everest goes up when someone chooses to hire an experienced guide or guide team to take on Everest."

What does a training regiment look like to tackle Everest – properly?

"You want to be physically fit, and have a certain amount of strength and power, but most importantly – on the physical side of things – you want to have a certain amount of endurance - a high cardio output and the ability to go for hours on end. Beyond the physical side of things you must have a certain level of mental fortitude to endure and enjoy – hopefully - the process of working hard on the mountain for that many days. People often see the summit as the end of the journey, and people make the mistake of letting their guard down mentally and their body physically, which is dangerous for the decent. What we work really hard to do is to prepare people for the duration of the entire endurance, the 65 days of climbing and trekking. On summit days specifically, to realize that the climb is to the top and back to our tent that day, and that getting to the summit is only the half-way point of the day."

How does a person get mentally ready for a challenge like Everest?
"The best training for climbing is climbing mountains, getting out as often as you can to work your body and exercise your mind and realize better systems and better ways for you to work towards that goal."

What's it like being on top of a mountain like Everest?
"I find it to be greatly humbling and inspirational at the same time. To see the curve of the earth from the top of a mountain, and to watch the sun rise from the highest point is absolutely magnificent and inspiring. Also reminds us of how small we are in comparison to all the other things that are going on and the natural beauty of the world. The summit is an amazing place to be, but it's the journey for me, from the planning and preparation before the climb, to the mountain, becomes the soul of the climb and the reason why I am there."

Thousands of our members have "to climb Everest" or even just "climb a mountain" as goals they hope to achieve in their life. For first time climbers, what's your biggest advice in getting started?

"First look online, there quite a few guide services that are very informative, like Alpine Ascents International. Mike Hamill wrote a guide book to the seven summits, called *Climbing the Seven Summits*, a really nice read on the 7 highest peaks on earth. And finally, find individuals who have some experience on the mountain, and use them as a resource."

Do you have any advice for first time climbers who want to get into climbing but don't know where to start?

"One of my first recommendations is to hire a guide with a lifetime dedicated to teaching, and helping people learn climbing and techniques on going into the mountain and back safely."

Tell us about the day you summited two 8000 meter peaks in one day? To any one of us mortals, climbing Everest peak would be more than a challenge. Did you set out to break the world record?

"I didn't think anyone had summited two 8,000 meter peaks in a day, but it wasn't until I confirmed with Liz Holly who manages the data-base for the Himalayan peaks after the climb that I confirmed it. It all started a few years ago when I saw a picture on my friend fridge from the summit of Cho Oyu where I later ended up climbing and have taken a very similar picture since, and as you look 25 miles from Cho Oyu towards Everest you see those peaks aren't so far apart. And it was looking at that picture on my friends refrigerator that I thought it would be amazing to climb one, come back down, and then climb the other in somewhat of a single push."

Since you've summited most of the world's most magnificent and challenging mountains, what is your favorite mountain to climb?

"You know I've climbed some of the most spectacular mountains in the world, and I've been asked that question a few times, and honestly I really don't have a favorite mountain. The mountain that I'm on becomes my favorite mountain."

DO EPIC SHIT

CONCLUSION

The best time to plant a tree was 20 years ago. The second best time is now. –Chinese Proverb

If I can impart any wisdom on you, it's that there is no time better than today to start working toward your goals.

> "You know, the ancient Egyptians had a beautiful belief about death. When their souls got to the entrance to heaven, the guards asked two questions. Their answers determined whether they were able to enter or not. 'Have you found joy in your life?' 'Has your life brought joy to others?'" – The Bucket List

So simple - life boils down to finding joy, and paying it forward.

Have you found joy in life?

Happiness is something we all strive to find and it's fundamentally part of all bucket lists – the pursuit of happiness. Always searching, growing and exploring to capture pure and utter bliss. Will it be in the person you've always dreamed of meeting, or the day you finally take off for your adventure around the world? Happiness is the secret to a successful life – or at least 50% of our purpose.

When we're growing up, often finding your purpose/passion in life and exploring your dreams is overlooked as a building block to becoming a successful – or at least functioning – adult. But it shouldn't be. At the end of the day when you love what you do, you'll become a better contributor to the overall well being of society. I can go on and on about why it's so important to 'find your joy' but a lot of people are probably asking how. And unfortunately a lot of things that contribute to happiness are out of your immediate control – i.e. time, money, and circumstance. But science has suggested that each individual is in control of about 40% of their own happiness.

> "A big chunk of how you feel is under your control, meaning the way you spend your time and the thoughts you allow to linger can really impact your mood and your long-term happiness … the point is that you can seek more positive interactions and take action to change the way you feel, regardless of your life circumstances.[48]"

And if that isn't appealing enough, check this out, the two biggest factors that contribute to happiness around the world are a sense of community & frequent community celebrations[49]. So essentially doing awesome sh*t with a good set of people will make you happy! I'm okay with that.

Has your life brought joy to others?
Secondly, and most importantly, in life, giving back has to be part of the foundation of who you are. Generosity is a part of

---

[48] http://www.happify.com/hd/happiness-by-the-numbers/
[49] http://cdn-media-2.lifehack.org/wp-content/files/2014/01/The-Science-of-Happiness-Infographic.jpg

human nature, because when we remove the focus from ourselves and instead focus on another, it's amazing what kind of gratification you receive.

So when the final grains of sand pass through the hourglass, I hope that you have done just two things with your life:

Find your joy, and find what you love to do
Pass that joy on to the people around you

And I couldn't end the book any better way than the wise, wise words of Arnold Schwarzenegger and his six rules to success.

1. Trust yourself

Many young people are getting so much advice from their parents and from their teachers and from everyone. But what is most important is that you have to dig deep down, dig deep down and ask yourselves, who do you want to be? Not what, but who. Figure out for yourselves what makes you happy, no matter how crazy it may sound to other people.

2. Break the Rules

Break the rules, not the law, but break the rules. It is impossible to be a maverick or a true original if you're too well behaved and don't want to break the rules. You have to think outside the box. That's what I believe. After all, what is the point of being on this earth if all you want to do is be liked by everyone and avoid trouble?

3. Don't Be Afraid to Fail

Anything I've ever attempted, I was always willing to fail. So you can't always win, but don't afraid of making decisions. You can't be paralyzed by fear of failure or you will never push yourself. You keep pushing because you believe in yourself and in your vision and you know that it is the right thing to do, and success will come. So don't be afraid to fail.

4. Don't Listen to the Naysayers

How many times have you heard that you can't do this and you can't do that and it's never been done before? I love it when someone says that no one has ever done this before, because then when I do it that means that I'm the first one that has done it. So pay no attention to the people that say it can't be done. I never listen to, "You can't." (Applause) I always listen to myself and say, "Yes, you can."

5. Work Your Butt Off

You never want to fail because you didn't work hard enough. Mohammed Ali, one of my great heroes, had a great line in the '70s when he was asked, "How many sit-ups do you do?" He said, "I don't count my sit-ups. I only start counting when it starts hurting. When I feel pain, that's when I start counting, because that's when it really counts." That's what makes you a champion. No pain, no gain.

But when you're out there partying, horsing around, someone out there at the same time is working hard. Someone is getting smarter and someone is winning. Just remember that. Now, if you want to coast through life, don't pay attention to any of those rules.

188

But if you want to win, there is absolutely no way around hard, hard work. Just remember, you can't climb the ladder of success with your hands in your pockets.

6. Give Back

Whatever path that you take in your lives, you must always find time to give something back, something back to your community, give something back to your state or to your country.

Arnold Schwarzenegger
Commencement Address
University of Southern California
May 15, 2009

ABOUT BUCKETLIST
The Action Network

Bucketlist is the global leader in bucket list inspiration, and motivation to achieve your life goals. Founded in 2011, the site has grown to over 200,000 members and 3,000,000 goals worldwide.

Bucketlist's Values

Bucketlist is an action network. We are a group of do-ers who thrive on living life to its fullest every day by checking things off our bucket list before taking off on our next adventure. It is a lifestyle.

We are about connecting with like-minded individuals to inspire and push each other to new limits. And through support from our community, even the big bucket list goals become achievable.

No goal is too big or too small to be on a bucket list. The most important thing is accomplishing each goal and living a fulfilled life.

At Bucketlist we are about taking action to live life. We are the **Action Network**.

Connect with Bucketlist

Create your free account at Bucketlist.org
Facebook - Facebook.com/bucketlist.org
Twitter - @bucketlistorg

Special thanks to Mackenzie Miller

Mackenzie is a writer from Buffalo, NY, USA who has traveled to over forty countries, mostly solo. She is always looking for new places and experiences to add, and then cross off of her bucket list. She shares her adventures on her blog, A Wandering Scribbler.

Mackenzie's top 5 bucket list goals:

1. Climb Mt. Kilimanjaro
2. Ride the Trans-Siberian Railway
3. Visit Antarctica
4. Watch the Northern Lights in Greenland
5. Volunteer at an orphanage in a developing country

Special thanks to Michelle Barber

Michelle Barber is a creative systems thinker living in Vermont, having spent time in Kentucky and Tennessee with origins in Detroit, Michigan.

Professionally, she's a digital marketer with a passion for non-profits, higher education, and the arts. Currently handling all digital media for the Vermont Foodbank, she spent the prior 10 years in higher education, most recently as the Director of Marketing at Vermont Technical College.

Michelle has also worked with non-profits ranging from large charity races (30,000 runners in downtown Detroit!) to non-profits and government agencies working with the youth, senior citizens, downtown development, the media, and poverty relief. She maintains a consulting practice around digital media for non-profits and small businesses.

Personally, she's an amateur adventurer and experiments in lifestyle design. She's kept a bucket list since she was 13 and recently committed to accomplishing 2-5 bucket list goals per year.

She's gone skydiving, hang gliding, and ziplining, gotten out of debt, and attempted a thru-hike of the Long Trail and a bicycle trip around the state of Vermont, among other goals.

Her top five bucket list goals, which haven't yet been attempted, or are in-process, include: learning how to rock climb, designing and building her dream home on a few acres of land, retiring early, young and healthy, learning to fly an airplane, and learning to sail.

RESOURCES

We discussed a lot of resources throughout the book. Here are our top bucket list websites and books to help guide your life.

Life Coaching and Bucket Lists
- Bucketlist.org
- EarlyToRise.com
- *Goals* by Brian Tracy
- Mindtools.com

Finance and Budgeting
- Budgetyourtrip.com
- Independenttraveler.com
- Lonelyplanet.com/travel-tips-and-articles/76405
- Mint.com
- Traveleye.com

Hotels and Accommodation
- Airbnb
- CouchSurfing.com
- Groupon.com

Hotels and Accommodation (Con't)

- Home Exchange
- Hotels.com
- Hotwire
- Kayak
- Priceline.com-

Flights

- Cheapoflights
- Flightfox
- Google Flights
- SeatGuru
- Skyscanner
- Traveleye.com
- TripAdvisor

Guides and Travel Communities

- The Backpacker
- Lonely Planet
- WikiTravel

Other resources

- Blog.bucketlist.org

- Budget Travel
- Cool Travel Guide.
- Perceptive Travel
- Travelvice

NOTES

NOTES

NOTES

NOTES

ABOUT SARA RUTHNUM

 Sara Ruthnum is a Digital Marketer and Community Builder for Bucketlist. She is committed to helping the world discover adventures and achieve kick ass goals.

Hailing from Regina, Saskatchewan, Sara moved to Vancouver, BC to attend the University of British Columbia – coincidentally the same year as the 2010 Vancouver Olympics. She now enjoys all the city has to offer, and is ready to explore and document all the micro-adventures in the city of Vancouver and beyond.

Sara received her Bachelor of Arts from the University of British Columbia with a double concentration in the Humanities and Economics.

Connect with Sara:

Email – sara@bucketlist.org
Twitter - @SaraRuthnum
LinkedIn – ca.linkedin.com/in/sararuthnum
Bucketlist – bucketlist.org/list/sara.ruthnum

KEEP UP TO DATE WITH
DO EPIC SH*T

Doepicshitbook.com

Facebook.com/doepicshitbook

Made in the USA
Coppell, TX
25 January 2022

72365929R00128